The Irrational Organization

Irrationality as a Basis for
Organizational Action and Change

Nils Brunsson
Stockholm School of Economics

FAGBOKFORLAGET

Copyright © 2000 by
Fagbokforlaget Vigmostad & Bjørke AS
All Rights Reserved

Printed and bound in Poland
by OZGraf SA

First published in 1985 by Wiley

ISBN 82-7674-570-9

Cover design by Fagbokforlaget

Distribution:
Denmark:
Munksgaard/DBK, Siljangade 2-8, P.O. Box, 1731, DK-2300 Copenhagen S,
Denmark
Phone: + 45 3269 7788, Fax: + 45 3269 7789

North America:
Copenhagen Business School Press
Books International Inc.
P.O. Box 605
Herndon, VA 20172-0605, USA
Phone: + 1 703 661 1500, Fax: + 1 703 661 1501
e-mail: Intpubmkt@aol.com

Rest of the World:
Marston Book Service, P.O. Box 269, Abingdon, Oxfordshire, OX14 4YN, UK
Phone: + 44 1235 465500, Fax: + 44 1235 465555
e-mail Direct Customers: direct.order@marston.co.uk,
e-mail Booksellers: trade.order@marston.co.uk

Inquiries about this text can be directed to:
Fagbokforlaget
Postboks 6050, Postterminalen
N-5892 Bergen
Tlf.: + 47 55 38 88 00 Faks: + 47 55 38 88 01
e-mail: fagbokforlaget@fagbokforlaget.no
http://www.fagbokforlaget.no

Contents

Preface

Writing a book is an action which requires irrationality to be started and some rationality to be concluded. Strong and unrealistic self-reliance is good for starting but at the moment of completion it is easier to be more realistic, realizing the importance of a benevolent environment. This book is the result not only of my own enduring interest in organizational decision-making, change and action. It is also the results of the efforts of many others. Members of the organizations studied gave generously of their time and patience. The ideas presented in the book also benefited from discussions with many colleagues. I wish particularly to mention Albert Danielsson, Walter Goldberg, Sten Jönsson, James March, John Meyer, Johan Olsen, Lee Ross and William Starbuck. During the spring of 1982 James March also provided for me at Stanford an excellent setting in which to complete most of the manuscript. Nancy Adler has worked hard to reduce the Swedish overtones in my English text. Anne von Tiedemann typed numerous versions of the manuscript. The Economic Research Institute at the Stockholm School of Economics has been a most co-operative employer, and the Swedish Council for Research in the Humanistics and Social Sciences has provided financial support. My thanks to all!

Stockholm, August 1984

Nils Brunsson

Introduction to the second edition: Decision-making as institution

In the modern world the individual and the organization are both expected to be rational. It is generally assumed that we would all be better off, were we only more rational. We ought to make decisions by predicting our preferences, examining all our action alternatives and all the consequences of these alternatives and then comparing preferences with consequences in order to find, and then adopt, the alternative offering the best consequences.

But we find it difficult to meet these expectations. Studies of the way individuals, groups and organizations make their decisions all show that deviations from the rational norm are routine. People use other forms of intelligence, apart from rationality: they follow rules, they imitate, they experiment. And even when we try to be rational, we often fail. Instead of looking at many alternatives and their consequences, we examine very few – sometimes even only one (Lindblom 1959); we base our decisions on our present preferences, even though we realize they may change later (March 1978); we assess consequences by rules of thumb, which are often highly misleading (Nisbett and Ross 1980); or we fail to act according to the decisions we have made (Brunsson 1989).

Such lack of rationality has almost always been regarded as a problem, and many explanations have been suggested for it. In this book a different, albeit related, issue is addressed: is it in fact intelligent to be rational at all? Maybe, after all, our lack of rationality is not necessarily a sign that we lack intelligence? Here it will be argued that irrationality may well be highly intelligent.

The ideas presented in the book were developed in the period around 1980. Those were the days when many students of organizations were questioning the common assumption that individuals and organizations are predominantly following an intentional and rational logic. It was argued that many social phenomena can be understood more fruitfully as instances of rule-following. Rather than choosing the action most likely to lead to their preferred and intended future state, people often follow rules. Instead of being guided by their ideas about the future, they are guided by their ideas of the past, by rules that already exist. Shared beliefs and norms often provide quite specific rules about what are the appropriate actions, and such rules then produce a similar pattern of actions among all those who share the beliefs and norms concerned. Special interest has been devoted to the broad, cultural systems of beliefs and norms and patterns of action that people take for granted; that is to say to social institutions (Berger and Luckman 1966, Jepperson 1991). Social institutions can be described as sets of very general rules which affect many people's actions in various social settings, thus explaining much individual and organizational action.

This general perspective is applied here to the analysis of decision-making in organizations and its consequences for action and change. Decision processes are shown to be instances of rule-following on two counts. First, there is a culturally based rule that organizations should make decisions at certain times, and decision-makers tend to follow this rule, at least in part. And further, instead of following the rational logic, decision-makers sometimes follow rules derived from local, organization-specific beliefs and norms.

An institution seen "from the outside"
Decision-making can be regarded as one of the central modern institutions closely associated with the fundamental institutions of the individual and the organization in their modern versions. Individuals and organizations are expected to make

many decisions. We expect their actions to be preceded by decisions, at least such of their actions as possess some importance and have not already become routine. It is assumed that by making decisions the actors are choosing their future actions. The whole idea of "decision-making" reflects the basic conception of individuals and organizations as autonomous actors, free to choose their actions and their futures according to their own specific intentions and preferences. The form of intelligence that best fits these conceptions is that of intentionality - we are supposed to choose actions that allow us to achieve our intentions in the future. The most appropriate logic for realizing this, is rationality. The idea of "decision-making" is thus associated with strong rationality norms. To put it another way, we could say that there is a cultural rule that individuals and organizations should be rational in a great many circumstances. Hence, paradoxically, in trying to be rational these actors actually reveal themselves to be following a rule.

Various perspectives are available to students of institutions. Much research is done from "within institutions", whereby researchers take certain basic institutional aspects for granted, just as other people in the same culture also do. Research conducted from this perspective includes studies of the way certain actors solve, or should solve, certain problems that are common since these actors tend to have certain interests and intentions in a given institutional setting. For example, this book looks at what makes organizations apt to change, something which has been regarded as a particularly important and difficult problem for organizations in turbulent environments. Studies from inside institutions have been seen as especially useful, since they concern what are generally regarded as major problems common to all and can thus perhaps come up with some solutions.

An alternative slant is to look at institutions "from the outside". This type of research is more likely to ask questions such as: why do certain kinds of actor emerge at all, why do they pursue their particular interests and intentions, why do they perceive certain problems, and why do they try to solve these problems in a certain way. Instead of taking institutional aspects for granted, scholars in this mould ask why certain things are taken for granted. A perspective "from without" is critical rather than useful.

There is a long tradition in decision-making research that adopts a perspective "from within" this institution. Here the beliefs and norms of the decison-making institution have set the research agenda. Scholars have shared the general, institutional assumption that decisions in themselves are intentional acts, and that the intention behind decisions is to make a choice from among future action alternatives. Both the cause and the effects of decisions have been assumed to involve choice: decisions-makers make decisions in order to make choices, and the essential result of decisions is in fact choice. Indeed, the terms "decision" and "choice" are regularly treated as synonyms. Scholars also assume that decision-makers are striving, or at least should be striving, to achieve a high degree of rationality. Deviations from the rational model are seen as failures, demanding an explanation. They are identified as the great standard problem of decision-making, and a vast body of normative resarch has emerged whose task is to help decision-makers to solve this problem, to help them in fact to become more rational.

The research agenda triggered by a perspective "from outside" the decision-making institution, on the other hand, looks rather different. Here it cannot be taken for granted that the cause and effect of decisions is choice of actions. We cannot even assume that there is necessarily always any relation at all between decision and action. We can expect to see decisions without actions and actions without decisions. The existence of decision-makers and decision-making is not taken for granted but is seen as the basis for research questions: what gets people to make decisions, when or in what situations are decisions made and when are they not, and what actions are preceded by decisions and which ones are not? Who are allowed and willing to act as decision-makers in various contexts, and what are the requirements, the incentives and ways of achieving the authority to perform the role. What are the effects of decisions, and are there other effects apart from action choices? What is the effect on decision-makers and decision processes of the very idea that decisions lead to choices? And what circumstances evoke a strong demand for rationality in decision processes, and in what circumstances are such demands less prominent? When do decision-makers strive towards rationality, and when do they seek to design their decision process according to some other tenet? What are the causes and effects of rationality and irrationality in decision processes?

Not all these questions will be posed, let alone answered, in this book. But the argument is based on this type of "from outside" perspective on decision-making. In contrast to basic institutional belief systems it will not be taken for granted that the cause or effect of a decision is a choice of action, or that decision-makers strive for any particularly high degree of rationality, or that they achieve it. In fact, the behaviour of decisions-makers in practice as described in this bok often deviates sharply from the standard beliefs about decision-making and from the standard norms.

Decisions, rules and rationality
The main observations in the book can be summarized as follows. The causes and effects of decisions do not necessarily correspond. A common cause of decision-making is that there is an institutional rule saying that decisions should be made. The effects of decision processes and decisions can be manifold. Decision processes may affect what action is chosen, but they may also affect the chances of the chosen actions actually being performed.

If decision-makers choose to stick closely to the rule regarding rationality, or if they have to do so, they are perhaps likely to make good choices, but they are also likely to come up against difficulties in realizing their decisions, since rationality tends to produce uncertainty which in turn can hamper co-ordinated organizational action. This last is vitally important to organizations which have been created for just such a purpose, i.e. to perform complex collective, co-ordinated, organizational actions. Mobilizing such actions is easier when decision processes are systematically irrational, for instance when decision-makers consider one action alternative only, and when preferences and consequences that support this alternative are the only ones considered.

Instead of adopting an intentional and rational logic, people sometimes employ a rule-following logic when they are choosing what actions to take. The rules concerned may have been produced by organizational ideology, i.e. shared ideas about the organization's situation and about the actions that are appropriate. If such an ideology is clear and precise and is shared by all the decision-makers - if it represents a kind of strong local institution - it can to a considerable extent dictate the choice of action. Since the choice is thus already made, any decision processes that are undertaken have other effects and can be used for other purposes. For example, they can be used for mobilizing action; since choice is not the purpose or effect of the decision, it is easier to avoid rationality and employ systematic irrationality.

These observations parallel earlier observations in social science about the co-ordinative effects of institutions on a societal level. Institutions that represent clear and widely shared ideas and rules, facilitate co-ordination and collective action in societies (Berger and Luckman 1966). If people's actions are guided by individual rationality rather than by common rules it becomes more difficult to mobilize co-ordination and collective action, and such action is then likely to occur only under certain specific circumstances (Olson 1965).

The recognition that rationality and action are difficult to combine has sometimes been used actively as an argument for rationality. For instance, the flag of rationality was raised by many of those who wanted to prevent any repetition of the kind of highly effective but evil organizational action that some states had achieved around the middle of the twentieth century. And rationality is also often advocated in more mundane circumstances, when people want to stop specific actions: a classic trick among oppositional groups is to try to obstruct or delay actions by trying to increase rationality in decision processes, by arguing that more preferences, alternatives and consequences should be analysed and taken into account.

Management perspectives
But when action is both vital and difficult to achieve, rationality is less useful or wise. It is sometimes rational to be irrational! From the analyses in this book it can be concluded that rationality is not likely to be a very intelligent mode for the "big" decisions involving complex co-ordinated actions with serious long-term consequences, while it may be so for the "small" decisions involving simple actions whose effects are primarily short-term. Action is facilitated by a specific kind of intelligence described in the book as "action rationality". Action rationality proves to be a combination of rule-following and systematic irrationality, and a more relevant term would perhaps be "action intelligence".

These arguments might seem to be making the question of change problematic. In a world of intentionality and rationality, change does not seem to be a much of a problem. Under changed conditions, the rational actor is supposed to analyse new prospects, make new predictions, reach new decisions and carry out these decisions out easily and according to intentions. Rule-followers seem to be more inflexible. Their aptitude for change is highly dependent on earlier changes in the rule system, e.g. that new rules have emerged or old ones have disappeared. If actions are governed by institutions, then fundamental changes in activities often require a change in the relevant institutions. If organizational actions are governed by organizational ideologies, then new kinds of action are promoted by a change in ideology.

But the dismantling of the old ideology is not enough. A state in which a disputed, confused or vague ideology holds sway, will not provide an adequate base for new organizational actions. Uncertainty about which institution is valid, or the lack of any institutional guidance at all, anomie, is not likely to produce much in the way of forceful collective action. Instead it is necessary to wait for new shared ideas and norms to emerge – a process that is not necessarily either very fast or easily manageable.

The rationality norm has a strong tradition in popular management theories (Furusten 1999). Managers are recommended to be more rational and more open to new ideas. And the more turbulent their environment, the more important it is to include new factors quickly in their rational decision processes and to try to challenge old ways of seeing the world. The main problem for management, and its foremost challenge, seems to be to think more quickly and better. Such ideas are infused with the dream that rationality and the quick adaptation of one's beliefs to new facts on the one hand and collective action on the other, can easily be combined - a dream that is popular in popular management theories as well as in other areas of modern thinking. It tends to be highly convincing to those whose only task is to think, and who do not need to mobilize collective action.

From this perspective the message in the book appears to be a pessimistic one. A further task and yet another problem are being attributed to managers - the task and problem of actually achieving co-ordinated and organized action. And what is more, the best way of solving this problem often contradicts the norms that tell us how to think better. Moreover both problems have to be solved in order to achieve change. In light of this analysis, management appears more difficult than the simpler rational account suggests. But it also seems more important and more challenging!

References

Berger, Peter L. and Thomas Luckmann (1966): *The Social Construction of Reality*. Garden City: Doubleday.

Brunsson, Nils (1989): *The Organization of Hypocrisy. Talk, decisions and actions in organizations*. Chichester: Wiley.

Furusten, Staffan (1999): *Popular Management Books. How they are made and what they mean for organizations*. London: Routledge.

Jepperson, Ronald L. (1991): Institutions, Institutional Effects, and Institutionalism in *The New Institutionalism in Organizational Analysis* edited by Walter W. Powell and Pul J. DiMaggio. Chicago: Chicaco University Press.

Lindblom, Charles E. (1959): The Science of "muddling-through". *Public Adminisration Review*, **19**, 79-88.

March, James G. (1978): Bounded rationality, ambiguity, and the engineering of choice. *Bell Journal of Economics*, **9** (2), 587-608.

Nisbett, Robert and Ross, Lee (1980): *Human Inference*. Englewood Cliffs: Prentice-Hall.

Olson, Mancur (1965): *The Logic of Collective Action*. New York: Schocken.

Chapter 1

Organizations and Change

ANY MANAGER WHO HAS BEEN KEEPING UP TO DATE with literature produced by both management researchers and management consultants over the last few decades, will probably have been left with the impression that the essence of good management is good thinking. Solving problems and making choices between alternatives are presented as the main management tasks, and a variety of complicated arguments, models and computer programs are offered as aids in finding the right solutions. To a quite overwhelming extent the advice given to managers has consisted of hints about how to solve problems in a more rational way.

At the same time descriptions of the way managers actually behave show that they spend very little time on problem-solving, decision-making or making choices, and when they do undertake any of these activities they tend to display considerable irrationality. This can be used — and often has been — as a justification for offering yet more advice about how to become more rational. But the same facts might suggest that rational decision-making is not after all the essence of good management. Successful management may have more to do with the ability to motivate people, to establish a good organizational climate, to create appropriate social networks, or to develop powerful organizational ideologies. The recent interest in Japanese management, which seems to be successful in these respects, is evidence of the spread of this type of approach.

In the present book the argument is taken one step further. It will be claimed not only that irrationality in decision-making and in organizational ideologies is a common feature of organizational life, but that it also has a highly functional role and is fundamental to organization and organizational action. Some organizations even have to learn how to

3

be more irrational, in order to survive in a tough environment.

The quest for irrationality ties up with the fact that in most organizations the main purpose and problem is not to effect thinking and choice but to produce organized, co-ordinated actions. But in striving for efficient action there is a great risk of organizations becoming inflexible. Inflexibility is in fact another fundamental attribute of organizations. It is therefore particularly difficult to achieve organizational action which is new and which involves big changes in earlier organizational behaviour. Such action poses not only a problem of co-ordination but also a problem of choice. In this book I shall describe how different kinds of organization deal with these two problems when trying to achieve 'action for change' and how various types of rationalities and irrationalities affect the outcome of their attempts.

1.1 ORGANIZATIONS AND CHANGE

Organizations exist to co-ordinate action and to achieve results which would be beyond the reach of unorganized individual actions. Both researchers and practitioners in the field have been eagerly looking for ways of making organizations into more efficient actors. And their efforts have not been in vain: productivity in relation to specific goals and at certain organizational levels has increased and is still increasing in many industrial organizations.

But when an organization is specifically designed to deal efficiently with one set of objectives, tasks and situations, problems may easily arise when it has to handle other objectives, tasks and situations. Efficiency seldom goes hand in hand with flexibility. Co-ordinating different people's actions also means reducing the range of actions available to each one of them. And while the reduction in variety may increase efficiency, it also tends to undermine the ability to promote new values, to perform new tasks or to handle new situations. For this reason many people are now asking how organizations can be made more flexible and adaptive.

Inflexible organizations cause problems in at least two ways. If an organization is in a very strong position either on its own or in co-operation with other organizations, it can effectively frustrate changes which are desired by people outside its own borders. Profound changes in societal values or in consumer preferences may not always lead to changes in organizational behaviour; in fact organizations may even try to influence people's values, to bring them in line with their own current behaviour. In this way organizational inflexibility can dilute the flexibility of the larger system to which the organizations belong.

If, on the other hand, inflexible organizations are unable to dominate the changing world around them, they will risk losing their legitimacy and their resources, and in the end they will probably die — greatly to the detriment of their own members and often to society as well, since the cost of allowing large organizations to die and replacing them by new ones can be very high. Structural unemployment during periods of rapid technological change is a case in point: in many instances it would have cost far less to have changed the existing organization in time.

In recent years it has become even more urgent for organizations to be flexible. There have been rapid changes on many fronts: in values, in the economy and in technology. An 'organization society' tends by its very nature to generate major radical changes in the organizational environment. The primary customers of a manufacturing company, for instance, will generally consist of a limited number of other closely interrelated companies, rather than an infinite number of relatively independent customers, and these companies in turn are becoming increasingly dependent on public agencies, local governments, unions, etc. A highly interrelated system of this kind, involving relatively few actors, seldom attains a steady state (Ashby, 1956): it is more likely to be characterized by turbulence in which changes are frequent and fairly extensive, and both they and their repercussions are difficult to foresee.

Organizational change has become a major subject of organizational research, together with various aspects of efficiency. The present book belongs to both these traditions. In studying organizational change, I became increasingly aware that this phenomenon can only be understood in light of the normal functioning of an organization, which both poses the problem of change and provides the conditions for solving it. I also found traditional individual-based organizational models inadequate when it came to analysing organizational change. In both descriptive and normative models the organization is often treated monolithically: it is assumed that it is dominated either by powerful entrepreneurs, as in microeconomic theory and much of the literature of strategic planning, or by dominant coalitions (Cyert and March, 1963); a single individual or group of individuals is supposed to wield complete control and to be able, through the agency of a strict hierarchy, to command and direct the actions of the other organization members. In other words action derives from the decisions taken at the top. In hierarchical models of this kind it is cognitive activities such as decision-making and problem-solving which are regarded as important explanatory variables, and the problem of change thus becomes a cognitive question only: all we have to do is to observe the need for change and to find out what change or changes to put into effect. But complex organizations can seldom be meaningfully described in these terms. The spread of industrial democracy suggests otherwise, as does the fact that even armies have problems with the motivation of their members. In the present book organizations will be described as consisting of numerous individuals, no one of which has complete control over the others when it comes to organizational actions.

Action as defined here includes activities other than the purely cognitive, and it cannot be expected to derive automatically from decisions, or choices, or problem-solving activities. Organizational action is accomplished by several organization members in collaboration. The purposes of organizational action require a reduction in behavioural variety and generate problems of change, but organizational change is also achieved as a result of organizational action. The relation between organizational action and change will be explained in greater detail in the next section.

1.2 ORGANIZATIONAL ACTION FOR CHANGE

Many organizations are created for the purpose of co-ordinated action. Indeed, some sort of organization is necessary when action calls for the collaboration of a number of people. But each one of these people will look at and interpret the various situations in his or her own way, and these differences will generate a huge potential variety of behaviour. The point of organizing is to reduce this variety in behaviour or potential behaviour. The existence of the organization ensures that its members will act within certain limits both now and in future, thus ensuring that they will be able to achieve joint action. The result of individual actions co-ordinated in this way is what we can call *organizational action*. Organizational action is at one and the same time the raison d'être of the organization and the cause of one of its main difficulties. The ability to achieve organizational action is not established now and for ever, simply because an organization has been created; the active maintenance of the organization is also vital. In a way the organization has to be recreated, before each new organizational action is undertaken: organizing is an ever-recurring activity of organizations.

Before it can act, an organization has to design rules delimiting the behaviour of the 'organized' individuals. At the least abstract and most concrete level, the rules consist of standard operating procedures for handling recurring situations — rules which are essential to the industrial production of goods, for example. Co-ordination is achieved according to a plan whereby each person behaves in a manner exactly specified in advance; the various actions combine to produce an organizational action. One of the most consummate examples of this type of rule is the assembly line.

Standard operating procedures can be formulated when the relevant situations and tasks can be specified in detail in advance. When this is not possible, the restrictions on behaviour have to be somewhat less stringent: roles can be substituted for standard procedures. A role provides a broader framework within which the individual can act. He can tackle a greater variety of situations, while his behaviour can still be predicted with some accuracy and it will still fit reasonably well with the behaviour of other individuals in other roles. Roles can be described as standard procedures at a higher level of abstraction: they represent more general rules for dealing with a more general class of situations. Roles may be tacit, having evolved gradually in interaction between people, or they may be specified explicitly as in job descriptions — for example, sales managers are to be responsible for marketing aspects of production,

production managers, for production aspects, and so on.

A third way of limiting the variety of individual behaviour is by influencing the way in which organization members perceive, interpret and evaluate events in their environment. Reducing conceptual variety thus represents an ideological method of co-ordination, and one which is at a high level of abstraction: it can also handle new situations. People who share a common ideology are likely to agree on the nature of a situation, and will probably have much the same ideas about how to tackle it.

All these methods for limiting the variety of behaviour in organizations thus create the capability to undertake co-ordinated organizational action. At the same time they produce considerable inertia: the powerful variety that the involvement of so many people could engender is not exploited, and the assortment of behaviours, perceptions and ideas which these people could express is drastically reduced. A major internal source of change is being blocked.

But external sources of change are also debarred. Environmental change tends, consistently, not to initiate change in organizational behaviour. If organizational action is to be possible, the immediate reaction to changes in the environment must be the conviction that they can be handled within existing procedures, roles and ideologies. This is an essential function of these instruments, without which they could not provide the means of organizational action. If they are to function as tools for the handling of the environment, their survival must not be threatened by that same environment. Inflexibility is one of the prerequisites of organizational action, and thus an essential feature of organizations as such.

Thus organizations achieve organizational action in a way that also obstructs organizational change. Solving the problem of action poses the problem of change.

And yet, organizational change is itself a form of organizational action. Organizational change means either that a new kind of organizational action is undertaken, or that a previous type of action is discontinued, or both. Change in the shape of cessation appears to be less problematic than change in the shape of new organizational action. Just like any previous actions, a new organizational action requires planning and co-ordination, but it cannot build on any existing organizing devices such as standard operating procedures. Instead it calls not only for organizational action, but also for the creation of a new set of organizing devices. The conditions for organizational action have to be created anew either before or during the action itself. It is this kind of *action for change* or *change action* which will be discussed in this book.

Thus any understanding of organizational change requires an understanding of organizational action, since the conditions of organizational action generate not only the problem of change but also the seeds of its solution. In the following chapters I shall therefore develop a theory of organizational action and apply it to an analysis of actions for change. First, however, a few words should be said about the kind of knowledge presented here and its practical implications.

1.3   THE STUDY OF ACTION FOR CHANGE

In the following pages organizational actions for change will be described and explained. Some of the main factors which promote or impede such action will be discussed and the relations between them examined. It will not be claimed, however, that any particular factors or processes are invariably important to every action for change. This kind of striving for generality is inappropriate in a social science, at least in connection with research at a deeper level. Claims to general validity beyond the limited section of reality and the point in time actually studied are necessarily unfounded and should therefore be avoided (Glaser and Strauss, 1968; Hägg and Hedlund, 1978; Brunsson, 1982; McKelvey and Aldrich, 1983).

Instead the main purpose should be to generate theories formulated for and based on specific social situations, which have been studied empirically. These theories form 'languages' that provide means for understanding the situations studied. Such theories can then be used by people involved in similar situations, when they are trying to improve their understanding of their own reality. Whether or not a given theory provides a useful instrument for understanding a specific situation can only be judged by someone familiar with that situation. Rather than generality, the basic empirical criterion for social theories is that they should make for a better understanding of the reality actually studied. This means that the demands on the empirical base are very exacting. In-depth case studies come to represent an important method and their presentation an important element in scientific reporting.

Thus, like all theories, the theory presented here is tied to its empirical base, and it should provide adequate explanations of the cases actually studied. But the main purpose is to provide hypotheses, suggestions and options for readers trying to understand situations familiar to them. The concepts developed below constitute a language which could be useful to an understanding of action for change in situations similar to those studied here.

The present study is concerned only with the actual process of change. External or internal triggers of organizational change have been extensively studied elsewhere, and will not be discussed here. The theory presented below has evolved from several case studies of action for change, most of which are described in the following chapters. Their sources include industrial companies, local governments and public authorities. Among the kind of changes studied are the development of new product and services and reorganization projects.

Action can be understood only in light of how the people concerned conceive of their situation. A great many in-depth interviews were therefore held with the key people in all the cases, with a view to charting individual actions and clarifying the participants' intentions, perceptions, and interpretations of the situations studied. Actions have also been studied by examining documents and sometimes by participant observation. The studies of the different organizations concerned lasted for anything from one to five years.

The order in which the results are presented below is not the order in which they were generated. The theory is propounded in a general form in Chapter 2. A presentation of the cases then follows. These are intended, first, to serve as a means of elaborating the theory, fleshing it out with more detail and making it more concrete, and secondly to show how the theory can be applied. Thirdly, the cases should provide an opportunity for the reader to check the validity of the theory against its empirical base.

Chapter 2

The Irrationality of Action and Action Rationality

I N THE PRECEDING CHAPTER I ARGUED THAT ORGANIZATIONAL action constitutes both the main purpose and the main problem of organizing. And yet much organization research has disregarded both the 'organization' aspect and the 'action' concept. Instead, research has been geared strongly to what can be called 'individual thinking'. Organizations have been treated as entities which behave in much the same way as individual people. The models used have often had a marked cognitive bias. Organizations have been described with the help of cognitive and individual-oriented concepts, such as learning and decision-making. The typical normative model focuses on ways in which managers can improve their analyses and decisions. The decision is often regarded as the equivalent of action; once we have learnt how to understand and predict decisions, we can also understand and predict actions.

2.1 THE DECISION-MAKING PARADIGM AND IRRATIONALITY

Much cognitively based organization research is primarily concerned with the problem of choice — how organizations choose actions, why they prefer one action to another — and choice procedures have popularly been described with the help of the decision-making paradigm. Organizational choices are said to consist of several decision-making steps, such as generating action alternatives, predicting the consequences of alternatives, and evaluating alternatives. The decision-making paradigm has been used both as a model for describing any choices made by organizations, and as an empirical concept describing a specific phenomenon. In the second case it is an empirical question whether or not a specific choice procedure can be described as a decision-making process, but

15

it seems as though the incidence of decision-making as an empirical phenomenon has been on the increase. People in organizations frequently describe their own activities as decision-making, and they try to follow the decision procedures as described in the model. This is probably to some extent due to the spread of the decision-making paradigm from theoreticians to practitioners, and this in turn is certainly due to the close association of the decision-making concept with the notion of rationality.

Researchers tend to evaluate decision-making processes in terms of rationality, and they have established norms for rational decision-making. In particular, great efforts have been put into prescribing how the 'best' choice should be made, given a specific problem, specific alternatives and specific information. Typically a problem is described as one where there is either too little information or too much. Less attention has been paid to other phases in the decision-making process, or the implementation of the decision once made.

Normative research has engendered an increasing consensus among researchers about the kind of decision-making that should be described as rational. At the same time empirical research has found ample evidence of decision-making processes that appear irrational by the normative standards (Lindblom, 1959; Cyert and March, 1963; Janis, 1972; Mintzberg, 1973; Tversky and Kahneman, 1974; March and Olsen, 1976; Nisbett and Ross, 1980). And what is more, these apparent irrationalities are not limited to minor decisions: people behave similarly when they approach major decisions on strategic issues. It can even be argued that the apparent irrationalities are greatest in the case of the weightiest decisions. Janis (1972) has described how decisions with serious or potentially serious effects, such as the Kennedy administration's decision to start an invasion at the Bay of

Pigs, were made without the benefit of normative rationality. Disturbing information was suppressed and illusions of unanimity were created among the decision-makers, who then took huge unjustified risks.

The irrationality that often informs decision-making is commonly explained in one of three ways. One chauvinist explanation is that the subjects studied are not clever enough to behave rationally. For instance, difficulties of implementing models from operations research have been explained by managers' emotional reactions or by their cognitive styles (Tarkowsky, 1958; Huysmans, 1970). If only decision-makers had the same knowledge and brain capacity as the scientists, they would surely behave as the rational decision models prescribe. Thus, decision-makers ought to be selected better and trained better.

A second explanation is derived from psychological studies which have suggested that certain types of irrationality are inherent in the human character, and are therefore difficult to change by any sort of training (Goldberg, 1968; Kahneman and Tversky, 1973). Therefore, not even experts can be completely rational; full rationality can be achieved only by mathematical formulae or computer programs.

A third way of explaining apparently irrational behaviour is by reference to practical constraints. In real-life decision situations, values and alternatives and predictions all interact, and decision-makers either possess incomplete information, or they have more information than any human being can grasp. According to this view, normative research should concentrate on designing systems for gathering and processing data, and indeed for a while many people believed that computer-based information systems would solve many management problems (Murdick and Ross, 1975). Also, recognizing that different objectives cannot always be readily compared, normative researchers have provided new tools in the shape of cost-benefit analysis and various multiple-criteria methods (Prest and Turvey, 1965; Keeney and Raiffa, 1976). These traditional explanations are firmly lodged in the decision-making perspective. They refer to diverse phenomena that disturb decision processes. Like the decision processes themselves, the disturbances are described in cognitive terms, as the result of deficiencies in perceived information or deficiencies in the mental abilities of the decision-makers.

None of these ways of explaining irrationality are wrong in themselves but there are good grounds for calling them inadequate: computer-based information systems have not been used in the prescribed ways; recommendations generated by operations-research models have not been followed; cost-benefit analyses have either not been undertaken or, if undertaken, have been neglected by even the most competent and successful managers and politicians (Churchman, 1964; Harvey, 1970; Ackerman et al., 1974; Argyris, 1977).

If real-world behaviour is to be understood, other explanations are needed; and so long as real behaviour is not fully understood, then the recommendations of normative research may be irrelevant, confusing or even harmful.

A decision-making perspective fails to recognize that managers do more than make decisions. Making a decision is merely a step towards taking action. The decision is not the end product. Managers get things done — act and induce others to act.

2.2 CONDITIONS OF ORGANIZATIONAL ACTION

When the focus of interest is shifted from cognition to action, a study of thinking is no longer enough. There is no automatic link between thought and action in organizations. It may be easier to trace the link between decision on the one hand and action on the other, if the decision-maker and the participant are the same person. It is very much more complicated and difficult when several decision-makers and several participants are involved, and when decision-makers and participants are not the same people. This is generally the case in organizations. Organizational actions naturally have a cognitive aspect, but other aspects must be taken into account as well before we can expect to understand such actions fully. Organizational action calls not only for cognitive processes or states but also for motivation and commitment.

An important cognitive condition of organizational action is *expectation*. If individuals are to find it worthwhile to act, they must believe that their doing so will result in an organizational action. And if they are to be able to co-ordinate their individual actions, they must all be envisaging the same end result. Present co-ordination is thus imposed by the future; it is the expected outcome of the individual actions, in the shape of an ultimate organizational action, that governs and co-ordinates the present actions. Organizations often try to evoke consistent expectations by formulating plans or decisions about future organizational actions. These instruments are frequently successful, but there is no guarantee that they will lead to the establishment of consistent expectations.

A second condition of organizational action is *motivation*, i.e. people's desire to contribute, through their own actions, to the resultant organizational action. Motivation is dependent on people's assessment of the action, on whether they regard it as good or bad. Thus motivation may be partly determined by choice or decision. At the same time it is in itself an essentially emotional aspect of action. Strong motivation is particularly necessary when there are powerful intellectual or physical obstacles. In such cases people will need a good deal of enthusiasm if they are to be able to complete the action. Both expectations and motivation are sensitive to uncertainty. If people are not sure whether a specific organizational action will actually be carried out, or if they are uncertain of its value, they will be less likely to undertake the individual actions which would contribute to its achievement.

A third condition of organizational action is *commitment*. This is the social aspect of action. In order to achieve something together, people must have some 'control' over one another, i.e. they must be able to rely on certain types of behaviour and certain attitudes in the rest of the team, before they will be willing to take part in the common actions. This control is secured by the creation of mutual commitment; people signal to one another their endorsement of any proposed action, perhaps by speaking in its favour or expressing confidence in its success. Commitment is also elicited from those who will subsequently evaluate the action, because committed evaluators are more likely to regard the action as successful (Brunsson, 1976).

The three conditions of action are not mutually independent. On the contrary, they can be expected to have a considerable effect on one another. For example, if people do not expect certain organizational actions to take place, they will be less motivated to act and will tend not to commit themselves.

The importance of the different conditions can vary with the situation, depending on such things as people's time horizons, the amount of change involved, and power relationships within the organization. Cognitive activities probably become more important where people expect more information to be beneficial. Motivation would be more important where people lack information needed for predicting the consequences of acting, where the negative consequences could be great, or where great efforts are essential; motivation would be less important where the actions are highly complex and people must collaborate extensively (Zander, 1971). On the other hand, commitment will be more important if a lot of people are involved, if the agreement of many parties is necessary, if efforts must be strictly co-ordinated, or if results depend upon the actions or evaluations of other people outside the group. Since motivation and commitment represent internal pressures for action, they are particularly vital when external pressures are weak, for example in wait-and-see situations when people think that it may be possible to take no action and they can reject one proposed action without having to accept another at the same time.

2.3   DECISIONS AS ACTION-GENERATORS

With the focus of interest on action, it is easier as well as more important to recognize that decisions can exist without actions and actions without decisions. Not all actions are preceded by the weighing of objectives, the evaluating of alternatives, or the making of choices; and decision processes and decisions do not always affect actions — particularly when the actions precede the decisions. On the other hand, decision processes often comprise some of the processes associated with action. And as managers and politicians both describe part of their work as decision-making, it is important that decisions and decision-making should continue to be studied.

It is in fact this very relationship between decision-making and action that can help to explain why decisions deviate from normative rationality. Since decision processes are aimed at producing action, they should not be designed solely in accordance with such intrinsic decision criteria as the norms of rationality: they should be adapted to extrinsic action criteria. Rational decisions do not always provide a good basis for appropriate and successful action. How, then, can decisions lay foundations for action?

Making a decision is only one of many ways of initiating action in organizations. But it is a very familiar one. Actions are often preceded by group activities, which are described by those taking part as decision-making steps. Some issue is posed in a form that allows it to be handled in a decision process: several action alternatives are suggested, their probable effects are forecast, and an action is finally chosen. Sometimes the decision-makers also formulate goals or other explicit criteria against which the alternatives can be judged. The final result is called a decision.

If a decision is to initiate an intended organization action, it must incorporate elements of cognition, motivation and commitment. Organizations should provide cognitive, motivational and social links between decisions and actions. A decision expresses the expectation that a certain action will take place: it also demonstrates a desire for the action (motivation), and it expresses the decision-makers' commitment to the specific action. Making a decision means accepting responsibility for the performance of the action and for its appropriateness.

The stronger the expectations, the motivations and the commitment incorporated in the decision, the greater the strength of the decision as a basis for action. In so far as the constituents of decisions are determined by decision processes, it will be possible to affect the probability of an action being realized by designing the decision processes. But effective decision processes break all the rules of rational decision-making; few alternatives should be analysed, only the positive consequences of the chosen actions should be considered, and objectives should not be formulated in advance. Irrationalities can provide a good basis for organizational actions in the following ways.

Searching for alternatives. According to the rational model, all possible alternatives should be evaluated. As this is impossible, the injunction is often reformulated and we are told to evaluate as many alternatives as possible.

In real life, however, far more decision processes appear to be geared to a limited number of alternatives (usually two) than to a large number. Even decision processes geared to single alternatives are common. Such parsimony makes sense in an action perspective, since the consideration of multiple alternatives often evokes uncertainty, and uncertainty reduces motivation and commitment. If people are uncertain whether or not a proposed action is a good idea, they are less willing to perform it or to commit themselves to promoting its success. Further, if people are not sure which action will actually be performed, they have to conjure up motivation for several alternatives at once, which dilutes the motivation attaching to any one of them. By the same token, commitment may be diluted or destroyed by the consideration of several alternatives. Thus at a very early stage in a decision process, if possible before it even starts, decision-makers should abandon any alternatives which have a slight or moderate chance of being chosen.

On the other hand, alternatives which have no chance of being chosen do not have these negative effects: they may even reinforce the motivation and commitment attaching to some other alternative. A common strategy is to propose alternatives which are clearly unacceptable, but which by comparison highlight the virtues of an acceptable alternative. This defines the situation as not being of the 'wait-and-see' type: rejecting one alternative means accepting another. A more important effect is that commitment operates in two directions, not only by the endorsement of acceptable alternatives but also by the disapproval of those that are unacceptable. Thus the consideration of two alternatives can provide stronger grounds for action than the consideration of a single alternative, if one of the two alternatives is obviously unacceptable.

Assessing consequences. Decision-makers who want to make rational decisions are supposed to consider all the possible relevant consequences of the alternatives proposed, the positive and the negative equally. But such a procedure evokes a good deal of uncertainty, since inconsistent information tends to produce bewilderment and doubt (Hoffman, 1968), as well as encouraging conflict among the decision-makers. And in any case it is difficult to weigh positive and negative consequences against one another (Slovic, 1972).

One way of avoiding uncertainty is to look for consequences in one direction only — to seek support for the opinions originally held about an alternative. People tend to latch their judgements on to the first cues they perceive (Slovic, 1972; Tversky and Kahneman, 1974). The search for the positive consequences of an acceptable alternative is given top priority, while any suggestion of negative consequences is suppressed. The purpose here is not only to avoid uncertainty; the active search for favourable arguments also helps to create enthusiasm and increase commitment to the alternative concerned. If negative consequences do impinge, the accumulation of yet more positive effects may help commitment and motivation to remain firm.

Evaluating alternatives. According to the rational model, alternatives and their consequences should be evaluated according to predetermined criteria, preferably in the form of objectives. Decision-makers are told to start from the objectives, and then to find out what effect the alternatives would have on them. This is a dangerous strategy from the action point of view, because decision-makers are only too likely to formulate inconsistent objectives and to find it difficult to assess the alternatives. Some of the necessary data may be difficult or impossible to find, and different pieces of information may point in contradictory directions.

A better strategy for achieving action is to start from the consequences and to invent the objectives later. Predicted consequences are regarded as good, because they can be reformulated as desirable objectives. The relations between alternatives and objectives are not investigated in detail; they are only examined sufficiently to demonstrate some positive links. Objectives are arguments, not criteria for choice; they are instruments of motivation and commitment, not of investigation. This is confirmed in situations when objectives disappear from the discussion as soon as it becomes clear that the preferred actions are not going to promote them.

Choosing. From the decision-making point of view, a decision is normally described as a choice automatically reached as a result of a preceding analysis. But when decision-making generates action, the choice is not merely the statement of a preference for one alternative; it is also an expression of a commitment to carry out an action. The choice can also be formulated in various ways, expressing different degrees of commitment and enthusiasm. And, finally, the question of who participates in the action is affected by who has participated in making the choice.

Making rational use of irrationality. The purpose of action calls for irrationality. Lindblom has argued that thorough rational analysis is irrelevant to the incremental steps in American national policy (Lindblom, 1959). But irrationality is even more vital to action involving radical change, because in such instances motivation and commitment are crucial.

Much of the 'decision irrationality' observable in decision processes can be explained as 'action rationality'. This hypothesis is particularly worth considering, in situations where motivation and commitment are highly desirable. Such an explanation could be applied to some of the strategic decisions described by Janis (1972), for example. Much of the irrationality observed by Janis in the Kennedy administration's decision to invade Cuba can be explained by the fact that such risky and normally illegitimate actions require very powerful motivation and commitment if they are to be adopted. Powerful motivation and commitment do seem to have arisen in the case of the Cuban crisis, and they resulted in determined efforts to complete action, despite great difficulties and much uncertainty.

According to Janis, better alternatives would have been found if the decision process had been more rational, allowing for more criticism, alternative perspectives, and doubts. Perhaps so. But deciding in a more rational way in order to avoid major failure is difficult advice to follow. If the decisions should generate action, then the irrationality is functional and should not be replaced by more rational decision procedures. Rational analysis is more appropriate where the benefits to be gained from motivation and commitment are slight — for instance when the actions concerned are less significant, less complicated, and geared to the short term. Lundberg (1961) observed that investment calculations are made when small marginal investments are being considered, but not when major strategic investments are being discussed. If one believes that rational decision processes lead to better choices, this observation should be disquieting. Moreover, powerful motivation and strong commitment tend to be attached to important actions, which makes it difficult to stop or change direction if the actions prove to be mistaken.

But there is also the opposite risk: that decision rationality can impede difficult but necessary actions. When action presupposes major organizational change, the magnitude of the issues and uncertainties involved may frighten people into making the most detailed analyses possible. At the same time, the uncertainty potential and the fact that many people are involved makes it even more likely that rational decision-making will obstruct action.

In the extreme and pathological case, people come to see decision-making as their only activity, ceasing to care about action or even to assume that any action will follow. In full accord with the decision-making perspective, they look upon the decision as the end product. Decision-making but not action can then be greatly simplified.

To sum up, rational decision-making procedures fulfil the function of choice—they lead to the selection of action alternatives. But organizations have two problems: to choose the right thing to do, and to get it done. There are also two kinds of rationality, corresponding to the two problems: *decision rationality* and *action rationality*. Neither is superior to the other, but they serve different purposes and are based on different norms. The two kinds of rationality are difficult to pursue simultaneously, because rational decision-making procedures are irrational in an action perspective. They should be avoided if action is to be more easily achieved.

How can the problem of choice and the problem of action be solved concurrently? One way is to solve the problem of choice with the help of ideologies rather than decisions. Ideologies can fulfil the function of choice without impeding action. This point will be elaborated in the following section.

2.4 IDEOLOGIES THAT FACILITATE ACTION

Researchers have recently been turning their attention to other cognitive aspects of organizational life than decision-making. They have pointed out that organizational members share certain interests which determine their participation in an organization. Further, the members entertain similar perceptions of the organization, of its environment, its history and its future, and some of their shared knowledge and attitudes may persist over a considerable period of time (Clark, 1972; Jönsson and Lundin, 1977; Starbuck, 1976; Starbuck *et al.*, 1978). Such cognitive phenomena, or certain parts of them, have been variously designated frames of reference, myths or strategies. In this book I will refer to them as *organizational ideologies*.

An ideology can be defined as a set of ideas; one person's ideas about a particular object or situation will be referred to here as a *cognitive structure*. Three kinds of ideologies can be distinguished in organizations. First, we have the individual cognitive structures of the organization members, which can be called *subjective ideologies*. Second, the members also have their own ideas about the cognitive structures of their colleagues, and these can be termed *perceived ideologies*, or what people think that other people think. Finally, *objective ideologies* are ideas shared by all organizational members, which provide a common basis for discussion and action. The different kinds of ideologies are to some extent at least inconsistent with one another.

Ideologies describe how things are and prescribe how they should be — two aspects which are often markedly interdependent, and both of which answer questions about reality. One question is '*How?*' How do organization members act in relation to one another or to people outside the organization? Another question is *'What?'* What has already happened (history), or what is going to happen (expectations)? Ideologies not only define what is perceived as fact, but also decide what facts will seem important. Further, ideologies can answer the question *'Why?'* Causes may be attributed to individual members or to the organization as a whole (self-attribution), or the surrounding world (environmental attribution).

Organizational ideologies are closely related to decisions, since they make it easier for people to agree on the objectives they want to pursue, on the action alternatives they see as promising, and on the outcomes they regard as probable. Ideologies permit short-cuts in decision-making, as they weed out some alternatives and consequences and enable decision-makers to omit or abbreviate certain steps (March and Simon, 1958). Ideologies can also replace decisions altogether: many organizational actions are not preceded by any decision process; agreement and co-ordination are achieved without decision-making, because the actors entertain similar perceptions of situations and share a stock of common expectations and general values (Danielsson and Malmberg, 1979).

Organizational ideologies tend to appear in organizations apparently quite spontaneously, but many organization theorists declare that they can also be intentionally moulded by the organization members (Ansoff *et al.*, 1976; Lorange and Vancil, 1977; Starbuck *et al.*, 1978). This suggests that ideologies could be formed for the specific purpose of avoiding rational decision-making, thus reinforcing the potential for undertaking difficult action. In fact, organizational ideologies can even reconcile thought and acting, since they can identify appropriate actions as well as contributing to their accomplishment.

If ideologies are to replace rational decision-making, then any confrontation between proposed actions and ideologies should lead to a clear result. It should be possible to classify a proposal as acceptable or unacceptable after very little analysis and discussion. There should be considerable consistency between the cognitive structures of individual organizational members. There should not only be common ideologies to underpin discussions, but these objective ideologies should be very conclusive — so clear and so narrow that any additional filtering of ideas would be unnecessary.

Conclusiveness could be attained if the objective ideologies included a limited number of precise normative statements. However, if any extremely simple ideology of this kind is confronted by a non-conformist action proposal, the ideology rather than the proposal might be called in question. Complex ideologies including contingency statements about an organization and its surrounding world can also be conclusive, and such ideologies are also less likely to be challenged by a single action proposal.

Ideologies which are conclusive, complex and consistent can provide a good basis for action, in that they solve a good deal of the choice problem. Such 'strong' ideologies can decide which actions are right, so that analysis is reduced to a minimum, and effort can be concentrated on reinforcing actions. Decision rationality can be applied to the creation of ideologies, and action rationality can be applied to the realization of actions. Thinking can be separated from acting.

The attribution of causes is also important. If action outcomes are thought to depend on environmental events, the organization should make forecasts of the type prescribed by rational models. If outcomes seem to depend on what members do within the organization, the crucial task will be to generate motivation and commitment. Thus, environmental attribution accords with decision rationality, whereas self-attribution accords with action rationality.

2.5 CONCLUSIONS

In this chapter two aspects of organizational thinking have been discussed: decision-making and ideologies. Observation of almost any organization will show that both these aspects tend to be irrational in the traditional sense of the word. Many decisions are based on biased information about a biased set of two (sometimes only one) alternatives, and the information is not properly weighted. An organization's ideologies focus the perceptions of its members on a few selected aspects of reality, and the confidence of the members in their own biased perceptions far exceeds what would appear to be justified. Organizational processes systematically reduce instead of exploit the multiplicity of perceptions that could have been fed into them by all their different members.

These irrationalities might appear both harmful and difficult to explain if the main purpose of the organization's thinking was to choose the right actions. However, the organization's main problem is not choosing; it is taking organized action. Decision-making and ideologies provide a basis for action, and they can be fully understood only if we recognize their function in this respect. Thinking must be adapted to the purpose of action; in light of this we can see that irrational decision-making and narrow prejudical ideologies are necessary ingredients of any viable organization that has to operate in a tough and complex environment.

Organizations face two problems in connection with action: finding out what to do, and doing it. When they are confronted with difficult actions, organizations separate the two problems. They solve the problem of choice by formulating ideologies; the various activities leading up to specific action can then concentrate on creating expectations, motivation and commitment.

2.6 TOWARDS A THEORY OF ORGANIZATIONAL ACTION FOR CHANGE

In repeating previous actions, organizations benefit from choices already made and action conditions already created. In the case of action for change, the problems of choice and action are both crucial. An action for change, or change action, first calls for an act of choice, since it is no longer a question of merely repeating past behaviour. But it also requires the creation of new expectations, motivations and commitment. And it will often evoke uncertainty, since previous experiences may be partly or wholly irrelevant. The choice–action dilemma is thus acute. A clearer understanding of the way organizations handle change actions should give us greater insight into both organizational stabilities and organizational changes.

The first fragments of a theory of organizational change actions have been suggested above. Several of the concepts and arguments presented call for closer analysis: what does an irrational decision process look like? What is meant by uncertainty and how does it arise? What do organizational ideologies consist of, and how are they related to organizational actions? But, to be fruitful, an analysis of this kind requires a closer link with empirical cases — a link which can also show how the concepts could be applied to real-life situations.

In the following chapters our present very general analysis will be pursued in greater detail, and we shall see how the concepts can be applied to real situations involving change in organizations. Each chapter thus contains two parts — a description of attempted change actions and a more detailed analysis of some of the main concepts relevant to the particular case.

The next chapter will describe two ways of making decisions which represent the categories rational and irrational decision processes. In order to understand their different impacts on the ability of organizations to undertake change actions, it is necessary to make a more detailed analysis of the concept of uncertainty.

Rational decision processes are a bad way of initiating actions. On the other hand, rationality may be demanded for other reasons. The case in Chapter 4 describes how an organization can avoid rationality when it is forced to adhere to the formal requirements of rational decision making. This case also provides good illustrations of the conditions of action since these were formed separately and were hence distinct. In particular, the commitment building process will be analysed.

Irrational decision processes are not appropriate for solving the choice problem of organizations. In this chapter it has been argued that organizations can solve the choice problem by ideologies instead of by decisions, thereby avoiding rational decision processes. Chapter 5 elaborates the concept of organizational ideologies and discusses the impact of ideologies on change actions. The qualities of ideologies that are most crucial in that function, namely ideological conclusiveness and consistency, will be specified and illustrated.

So far change actions which are consistent with existing organizational ideologies have been discussed. But how do organizations undertake more radical change actions which are inconsistent with existing ideologies? In Chapter 6 it is argued that such actions require ideological change and that different types of ideological change benefit from different types of organizational ideologies. Strong ideologies make organizations 'changeful', weak ideologies make them 'changeable'.

One of the main implications of the action perspective is that organizational change actions are particularly difficult in political organizations—organizations which institutionalize conflict and strive for ideological inconsistencies. This is discussed in Chapter 7.

The theoretical discussion in Chapters 3 to 6 is structured round the cases. In the final chapter, the theory of organizational change actions is summarized according to its own logic, and some implications are discussed.

ACKNOWLEDGEMENT

This chapter is a revised and shortened version of the author's article 'The irrationality of action and action rationality: decisions, ideologies and organizational actions', *Journal of Management Studies*, **19**, 1, 1982, p. 29–44, and is reproduced by permission of Basil Blackwell Publisher Ltd.

Chapter 3

Rationalities, Uncertainties and Actions

I N THE LAST CHAPTER IT WAS ARGUED THAT EXPECTATIONS, motivation and commitment are major conditions of organizational actions. Motivation and commitment will be analysed in greater detail below, while the shaping of expectations will be discussed in the following chapter. But motivation may be severely undermined by uncertainty, and since change actions render at least some aspects of previous experience obsolete as a basis for judging the future, they are only too likely to produce uncertainty. The whole question of the relationship between uncertainty and change actions and how the one affects the other is therefore of particular interest.

In this chapter the concept of uncertainty will be explored in greater depth. Rational and irrational decision processes and their effects on uncertainty will be described in some detail. Relationships between uncertainty and expectations, motivation and commitment will also be discussed.

3.1 UNCERTAINTY

A subjective concept of uncertainty

Uncertainty is one of the most frequent concepts in organization theories. This does not mean that it is always important. The concept has often been used to describe states of the world outside the individual rather than states of mind of individuals (Downey *et al.*, 1975). The concept can then be replaced by other concepts describing the environment, such as variability or complexity. Such a use of the term means that the potential of uncertainty as an explanatory variable is far from fully exploited. A more powerful way of defining uncertainty is to let it describe a 'psychological state' (Downey and Slocum, 1975).

Even if we accept the psychological definition of uncertainty, there is room for several more detailed definitions. According to one common type of definition, uncertainty is lack of information. Downey and Slocum (1975) proposed the definition 'that uncertainty exists when an individual defines himself as engaged in behaviour based on less than complete knowledge of existing and future relations between the individual and his environment and how these are casually related to each other'. Uncertainty can then be measured by asking people how often their information about a variable is incomplete, or how often they find that they do not know what to expect of it (Duncan, 1972; Nebeker, 1975). But it is not clear what these authors mean by 'knowledge' and 'information'. Knowledge and information can be defined as *correct* knowledge and information. If this definition is accepted, then it will be natural to describe uncertainty simply as lack of information. If information is defined as correct information it is impossible by definition to obtain any information about the future and, strictly speaking, anyone who sees future events as an important factor in determining present action is thus going to be constantly uncertain.

But knowledge and information can also be defined so as to allow for the possibility of their being incorrect (Boulding, 1966). Hints, guesses and forecasts are also information. Uncertainty can thus be supposed to be related to the incorrectness of information as well as to its incompleteness.

People use estimations and guesses as bases for decisions and actions. Uncertainty refers to the degree of reliance which they place on those pictures and guesses about the past and the future that they actually use in their thinking. Uncertainty is thus a lack of confidence or belief in our own cognitive structure of a situation (Nyström, 1974): people are not certain whether their cognitive structures are an adaquate reflection of the situation.

It is lack of confidence in existing information which is the main source of uncertainty, not lack of information. Lack of information is only an extreme, special case of uncertainty.

People's confidence in their own guesses may vary but there is no reason to believe that they always or often lack confidence. Uncertainty is not necessarily a common phenomenon, even in organizations which operate in changing and complex environments. The fact that external researchers feel uncertain when they observe such environments and try to assess their future, is no proof that the organizational actors feel uncertain. Introspection as a research method has definite limits. On the contrary, there are several studies of individuals which suggest that people are 'overconfident' (Nisbett and Ross, 1980). Beliefs in organizations are often much stronger than seems justified even when organizations are exposed to new and contradictory information (Sproull, 1981).

Different theories relate uncertainty to quite different objects. Some studies, as we have seen, relate it to the organization's environment in general. Measurements often concern people's uncertainty regarding specific variables (Duncan, 1972; Nebeker, 1975; Leifer and Huber, 1977). But different tasks (Galbraith, 1977) or actions can also generate varying amounts of uncertainty within an organization. Moreover, people may feel uncertain about their general environment or about the value of specific variables and yet feel no uncertainty when faced with specific actions, or vice versa. Obviously action-related uncertainty is what is relevant to studies of organizational behaviour.

The desirability of actions can be judged by their consequences and by their consistency with norms and rules (March, 1978). Since consequences belong to the future, there is no definite way of assessing them; judgements of consequences can be expected to have a relatively high potential for generating uncertainty, in general higher than judgements of consistency with norm.

Types of uncertainty

In Chapter 1 it was argued that the organizational actions for change were not co-ordinated by standard operating procedures. Since they are actions geared to change, they cannot be justified by reference to their agreement with existing rules. Instead they can normally be expected to be judged by their consequences. Uncertainty is then connected with the assessment of these consequences and of their value ('good' or 'bad'). Purposive actors like to base their actions on some ideas about what reality will look like with or without their actions, or about the effect their actions will have on reality. These ideas stem from the actors' perceptions of the relevant situation, i.e. from their cognitive structures. More specifically, the cognitive structures consist of people's selective perceptions of different parts of their environment and their understanding of the causal relationships between them. The cognitive structures also incorporate values (i.e. ideas of what is good or bad). Starting from this model it is possible to distinguish several kinds of uncertainty, which can be expected to stem from different sources or to lead to different effects.

Uncertainty in cognitive structure is the most comprehensive kind of uncertainty. The individual is uncertain whether his cognitive mapping as a whole represents a valid picture of reality. Perhaps he is not sure whether the parts of reality which he discerns are in fact the most crucial, or whether his assumptions about their causal interrelations are correct. An extreme case of uncertainty in cognitive structure occurs when the individual almost lacks any cognitive structure at all — when a situation has arisen, so new and unfamiliar that it is not even possible to make vague guesses about what is important or what will happen. This is the special case of incomplete information referred to above.

Judgement uncertainty. A person may also experience uncertainty in relation to the normative area of his cognitive structure. He may be uncertain about the values he wants to attain, so he is not sure whether a given action is in fact good or bad, even if he is certain about its effects. A less extreme variety of judgement uncertainty may arise when an action is perceived as affecting various values in opposite ways, some positively and others negatively. If the person is ignorant or uncertain about the relative status of each value, it will be difficult to judge the action.

Estimation uncertainty. Finally, a person may be uncertain about the correct estimation of a given descriptive element in his cognitive structure. An investor for example, may be certain that the market for a product is an important factor, and there may be no difficulty in weighing the market aspect against the investment cost. But there may still be uncertainty about whether or not to invest, if the investor is not sure about the future size of the market for the product. This is the kind of uncertainty which is most frequently discussed in economic literature. Here it will be referred to as estimation uncertainty.

Effects of uncertainty

Uncertainty affects motivation. People who are uncertain whether the consequences of an action will be good or bad cannot be expected to feel as highly motivated as those who are certain of the action's desirability. Diminished motivation reduces the propensity to act. Substantial uncertainty can effectively hinder action, at least so long as the non-action alternative is perceived as possible.

Uncertainty in cognitive structure is of fundamental importance in the sense that it leaves the outcome of the action completely open. If the world is not as I have guessed, then anything is possible; my action may equally well result in disaster or success. This is unlikely to inspire motivation, and the situation may well be aggravated by further uncertainty: the person is not sure whether any modification in his action will affect the outcome, and if so how. As the cases in this chapter will show, uncertainty in cognitive structure can even have immediate negative consequences on the propensity to act; it may be difficult to envisage any possible action or to establish criteria for specifying actions in greater detail — particularly in the extreme case when the person possesses no relevant cognitive structure at all.

Judgement uncertainty is similar to uncertainty in cognitive structure in the sense that it involves the person in conceptual or logical difficulties. Uncertainty in cognitive structure makes it difficult even to start considering an action; judgement uncertainty makes it difficult to complete its consideration. In neither case can uncertainty be reduced by seeking and adding 'better' information about certain specific elements in the cognitive structure. For example, it is no use waiting for predicted elements to materialize as facts. Uncertainty in cognitive structure can only be reduced by greater general knowledge or familiarity with a particular reality, and judgement uncertainty can be reduced by a clearer conception of one's own preferences.

Estimation uncertainty is connected with difficulties in assessing the possible effects of an action. These difficulties are empirical rather than logical. An individual can reduce his uncertainty by searching for better information about elements which are causing uncertainty. Estimation uncertainty does not necessarily affect motivation. Direct influence can be expected in two cases only: first, if it seems possible that the values of some elements may deviate so markedly from the anticipated values that the action would not have been undertaken had the values been known for certain; second, if it seems possible that the values of some elements might prove such as to have engendered judgement uncertainty, had they been known earlier. In other words, estimation uncertainty does not affect motivation when the person has no doubts about undertaking the action, even if the elements should be discovered to have the worst (or best) values envisaged.

Risk

Uncertainty thus affects motivation. But in order to understand the full impact of uncertainty it is necessary also to consider the concept of risk. Risk, as the term is used here, is the product of the uncertainty experienced by the individual and the stakes— or possible net losses—involved in the action. Since risk is defined as the product of 'uncertainty x stakes', there can be no risk if either one of these is absent. Risk represents a greater threat to motivation than mere uncertainty. Risk reduces the motivation for a given action by providing a 'contra-motivation', i.e. motivation *not* to undertake the action. The balance may even swing in favour of non-action.

What constitutes stakes in organizational actions?

In most organizations the motivation of individual members can generally be expected to depend at least partly on their estimation of the effect on themselves of a given action. These personal consequences will usually be related to the effects on the organization as a whole, but they are not identical with these. If an action proves to have negative consequences for the organization, only under certain circumstances will it have negative effects for the people who took part in the action. If the action results in a severe threat to the existence of the organization, then the position of the individual organization member will of course be at risk. But if the negative effects are less marked, their importance to individual decision-makers will depend on the extent to which the decision-makers are held responsible for the negative effects.

The individual decision-maker's stake is determined by his responsibility for the effects of his actions on the organization. Responsibility provides the link between the effects for the organization and the effects for the individual. But many factors normally come into play here, which serve to reduce the negative effect on the decision-makers considerably in comparison with the effects on the organization. For instance, it is usually difficult to establish incontrovertibly that certain events are due to specific actions; further, events may have occurred which are accepted as being impossible to foresee; and, finally, up to a point mistakes are regarded as justified and the idea of a 'normal' business risk is accepted in most business organizations (Aharoni, 1966).

The distinction between risk and the various types of uncertainty will be germane to the following discussion of the relations between rationality and uncertainty. If the risks are severe, it is much more difficult to create high motivation for an action. From our empirical studies of change actions, no conclusion can be drawn about the relative impact on motivation of risk or mere uncertainty. But observations of the great efforts which actors made to reduce risk suggest that risk was an important factor.

3.2 RATIONALITIES AND UNCERTAINTY

A great deal of the discussion of sources of uncertainty has focused on characteristics of organizations' environments. But uncertainty can also stem from internal sources, for example from the way people perceive and react to external situations. Decision rationality is one such internal source of uncertainty. In the following pages a rationalistic decision process will be compared with a non-rationalistic process, and the likelihood of decision rationality giving rise to uncertainty will then be demonstrated.

Decision modes

The decision processes to be used in the illustration below have been taken from a study of the way in which decisions on product development projects were reached in two companies, and how this influenced the companies' ability to launch products which differed radically from their existing range (Brunsson, 1976). In the industry to which the companies belonged, product development projects generally involved quite difficult organizational change actions. Such actions required the co-ordinated efforts of many organization members. In order to develop new products successfully it was necessary to undertake demanding laboratory research, as well as to test the product both in the production system and on the market. This meant that many people at different levels and in different departments in the company had to be motivated to take part, even if this involved serious disturbances in other important tasks and even if the future success of the project sometimes seemed doubtful. It was necessary to elicit commitment from a great many people throughout the organization.

A very high level of motivation was needed among those managing the project. All the people agreed that enthusiasm was a necessary part of product development work. Enthusiasm made people willing to invest the time and effort needed to give a project a good chance of success. Enthusiasm also made it easier to decide to start new projects.

Strong motivation was needed partly because there was little external pressure to decide on specific new products or to realize a project once it had been accepted. Decisions about whether or not to develop new products generally entailed a perfectly realistic non-action alternative. It was quite possible to reject a project proposal without simultaneously proposing or accepting another. No specific customer was impatiently waiting for the work to be completed. Enthusiasm provided the internal pressure that made it possible for the project to compete with other activities exposed to stronger external control (for instance, the production equipment was needed for products specifically ordered by customers).

Product development activities can be expected to have great potential for the generation of uncertainty. Whether uncertainty actually occurs will depend on the decision processes involved, as the following description of the decision-making modes used in two companies can illustrate. The modes are extremes in the sense that they represent two sets of opposing characteristics.

The first mode provides a concrete example of what we have called decision rationality (see Chapter 2). It resembles the customary recommendations of normative decision theory and can be described as an ends/means analysis. The idea was to assess the possible effect of an action on come of the decision-makers' general goals. Various factors, essentially the same for all new product decisions, had to be analysed to establish what the effect would be. Since the purpose of introducing a new product was to increase profitability, the future sales volume of the product, its possible price, and the production costs all had to be estimated. The estimation of each of these factors then required that the values of various other factors were assessed, and so on. It was a question of filling a given structure with estimated values (see Figure 3.1) where the values were ultimately dependent on the concrete qualities of the project under consideration. This is what we can call the rationalistic mode of decision-making. It contains much decision rationality.

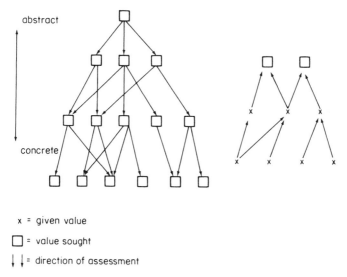

abstract

concrete

x = given value

☐ = value sought

↓ ↓ = direction of assessment

Figure 3.1   Two decision-making modes

However, the rationalistic mode is not the only way of making decisions. Another company in the same industry and involved in similar product development activities approached its project decisions in the opposite way, using what can be called the impressionistic mode. This company's decision processes started from one or two concrete attributes of the project under consideration — attributes which could be regarded as 'good' or 'bad'. The sum of such attributes determined whether or not action should be taken. Abstract concepts like profitability were still used, but now as arguments for the 'goodness' or 'badness' of an attribute and not as points of departure for the evaluation (see Figure 3.1). Further elements were added in support of the conclusion drawn from the first attributes considered: if these had indicated that the action was a good one, then further positive elements would be looked for; if the first attributes were negative, other negative elements would be sought. The impressionistic mode contains a good deal of action rationality, as we shall see below.

It was found that the two decision modes produced quite different degrees of uncertainty. The decision-makers using the rationalistic decision mode reported a lot of uncertainty in their consideration of product development projects. In most cases they were uncertain whether the proposals would lead to successful products or not. The decision-makers using the impressionistic mode reported no uncertainty except for a few proposals which were so unlike the usual cases that the impressionistic decision-makers felt unable to assess them at all. No such uncertainty was reported by the rationalistic decision-makers. To use the terms defined above, the decision-makers applying the impressionistic mode reported a few cases of uncertainty in cognitive structure while the decision-makers applying the rationalistic mode frequently reported uncertainties of all kinds except in cognitive structure. These are natural effects of the different decision modes employed.

The two modes require a different level of familiarity with the kind of action being considered. Decision-makers following the impressionistic mode have to start from certain attributes of the action and they have to be able to determine whether these are good or bad. They find it difficult to assess actions in areas with which they are not familiar. The rationalistic decision-makers have no such difficulties, since they make their assessment on the basis of a model general enough to apply to almost any action where the objectives are relevant. Starting the assessment from the objectives is like starting from one's own qualities, with which one is familiar and which are stable over many consecutive actions.

However, the rationalistic mode has high potential for producing other kinds of uncertainty. Estimation uncertainty will obviously attach to all the necessary assessments of the various factors. Values are often very difficult to predict. There will generally be some elements which are expected to have a positive impact on the ultimate objectives and others expected have a negative impact; it may then be difficult to assess the net effect on the objectives, and this can give rise to judgement uncertainty.

The impressionistic mode has very low potential for generating estimation and judgement uncertainty. There is no problem about estimating the values of the elements; people use elements whose values are obvious, or to put it another way, they make their assessment on a basis of given values, not on a basis of elements into which values are to be inserted. When abstract elements are used, their values are not estimated; instead they are used to underpin the values chosen as criteria. Since new elements are added to support opinions already formed, the possibility of judgement uncertainty is substantially reduced.

Thus the impressionistic mode may cause difficulties at the start of assessing a proposal for change into an area within which the actors are unfamiliar. On the other hand, if the assessment is actually performed, the impressionistic mode has almost no potential for generating uncertainty while the rationalistic mode possesses great uncertainty potential. Decision rationality and uncertainty are intimately related.

3.3 RATIONALITIES, MOTIVATION, COMMITMENT AND EXPECTATIONS

Risk reduction and motivation

If the risk is perceived as high, people feel less motivated to act and may even refrain from action altogether. Sometimes they find they have to act despite the risk, i.e. non-action is regarded as a far worse alternative than action. Various measures may be taken in order to reduce the risk. Perhaps the search is intensified for a less risky alternative action, for example one involving less cost or quicker returns.

Another way of lessening the risk is by modifying an action so as to reduce the possible negative effects on the organization. A common strategy is to break the action down into several smaller steps, which makes it easier to stop at any of several stages without having invested too many resources. Each step also involves a smaller stake on the part of the decision-makers. As the participants proceed, their overall responsibility for the action accumulates and their stakes may approach successively more critical levels. On the other hand, the uncertainty may diminish with time, when it becomes easier to forecast the final result. The total effect may be to keep the risk at an acceptable level. This is the idea behind pilot projects, marginal reforms and incremental changes.

But it is also possible to reduce risk without modifying an action. Since risk is the product of uncertainty and stakes, it is possible to diminish the risk involved in any given action by reducing either the uncertainty or the stakes.

It may be possible to reduce the uncertainty factor by trying to learn more about the probable effects of the action, although this solution has its limitations. It often means trying to predict future events resulting from highly complex cause-effect relationships in a social system. By definition information about the future is unattainable: what we have is information about past events from which we might be able to form hypotheses about the future. And relevant past events are particularly hard to find when the actions under consideration are concerned with change.

The other approach to the risk problem is to try to reduce the stakes involved. Decision-makers can actively reduce their responsibility for a decision, and thus the risk which they take. When the negative effects of the action appear, they may argue that these could not have been foreseen or that they are within the limits of 'normal' risk-taking. When they actually make the decision, the decision-makers can assess their future ability to convince others by these arguments, and if the outlook in this respect appears good, then both their responsibility and hence the risk can be regarded as fairly slight. But the risk is not usually as small as it would have been if they had abstained from action; it is usually easier to establish the failure of an action that has been performed than to argue for the hypothetical success of an action that has never taken place.

When decisions are made by a group of people, responsibility can also be diluted by being shared among several individuals. This may be one reason why groups sometimes accept greater risks than individuals (Wallach et al., 1962 and 1969, Bem et al., 1965). Once total responsibility has been reduced as much as possible, the remainder can be shared among the decision-makers. There are several ways in which people can evade responsibility without directly arguing in favour of non-action. They may express uncertainty by pointing out some of the drawbacks of the action. Or they may make it clear that their acceptance is only temporary and that it might be withdrawn later when the action has been started and some experience has been acquired. Evasive moves of this kind increase the responsibility and risk of the other decision-makers, however, and make it more difficult for the group as a whole to agree on the action. Thus, at least in a group context, it is better to reduce risk by reducing uncertainty than by reducing responsibility, if motivation is to be promoted.

But, in the context of motivation, there is a further reason for preferring a strategy of uncertainty reduction. Less responsibility means less credit, should the action prove to be a success, whereas great responsibility also brings more credit. At the same time a low level of uncertainty means that people believe more firmly in success, while a high level of uncertainty means that they consider failure to be quite likely. Thus, those who reduce risk by reducing uncertainty while accepting responsibility, are fairly convinced that their responsibility will bring them credit. Those who reduce risk by reducing responsibility while maintaining a high level of uncertainty are fairly sure that their responsibility will bring discredit upon them. Uncertainty-reducers are speculators in success: stake-reducers are speculators in failure. Uncertainty-reducers must normally be expected to be more highly motivated.

Risk reduction, commitment and expectations

To sum up, although the two methods of risk reduction may lead to the same low risk level, they are not equivalent in an action context since they tend to generate different degrees of motivation. Added to this, they tend to produce different levels of commitment and expectation. Not only risk but also commitment and expectations are dependent on responsibility.

'Commitment' means that a person is regarded by other people as being clearly tied to a specific action. The ties must be perfectly evident to others, explicit and 'strong', if they are to persist through the effort and energy required to overcome the foreseen and unforeseen difficulties that are typical of change actions. Participation in decisions and decision processes represents an important device for ensuring commitment, although the strength of the commitment itself can vary. Commitment can be the result of explicit promises to endorse and participate in an action. But people may also become committed by assuming responsibility for the action concerned. Acceptance of responsibility is a way of signalling one's support for an action to other people. A person who has accepted responsibility for an action will be expected by others to feel responsible and to behave accordingly, i.e. to contribute vigorously to the successful completion of the organizational action in question. Thus the acceptance of responsibility also helps to strengthen expectations that the action will in fact be performed.

Individuals can avoid responsibility by not participating in the decision or by clearly declaring their opposition to it. In this last case they are assuming a kind of negative responsibility: they will be blamed for their bad judgement if the action is performed and turns out well. As we have already seen, however, there are several ways in which decision-makers can evade responsibility without openly rejecting the proposed action. The evasion of responsibility inhibits commitment and expectations, thus reducing the oppportunities for organizational action.

The two rationalities and risk reduction

Decision modes do not only influence uncertainty; they also affect responsibility. The rationalistic mode provides ample opportunity for evading responsibility: it can be used by people who want to emphasize the uncertainty of some of the estimations, particularly those referring to rather abstract elements, or by anyone wanting to draw attention to the pros and cons inevitably attaching to a proposal. The fact that it becomes fairly easy to evade responsibility is important to the individual, since this decision mode also tends to produce the second risk factor, namely uncertainty. Thus, a rationalistic decision mode offers both a need for responsibility evasion and a method for achieving it.

The impressionistic mode, whereby arguments are gathered in favour of accepted actions, provides a way of achieving considerable responsibility. At the same time it tends not to generate uncertainty, and so the decision-makers have no reason to evade responsibility. The impressionistic mode also offers a good basis for the generation of keen motivation. No uncertainty and a high level of responsibility for oneself and others can arouse considerable enthusiasm for an action among those involved. Motivation is easily killed by a decision mode which generates uncertainty and evokes little responsibility.

These effects can be greatly reinforced by the interaction between motivation, expectations and commitment. A low level of responsibility and a high degree of uncertainty produce little or no commitment, which in turn means little or no positive expectations and further a reduction in motivation, and so on.

The effects of the different decision-making modes in the two companies studied were very striking. In the company employing the rationalistic mode, there was much uncertainty but little responsibility or commitment and a low level of expectation. The decision-makers tended to reject any proposals for new products that might involve big changes in the present product range, although there was general agreement that the company needed new products of this kind. In the company employing the impressionistic mode no evasion of responsibility could be observed, and development work was pursued with obvious enthusiasm. The company succeeeded in accepting and realizing projects for new products that involved radical changes.

Figure 3.2 provides a summary of the arguments outlined

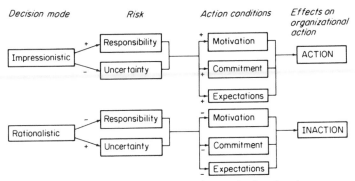

Figure 3.2   Decision modes and organizational actions

above. Both decision modes can be used to reduce the risk involved in an action. The impressionistic mode dilutes the potential risk by reducing the uncertainty. The rationalistic mode generates a high degree of uncertainty, but it also dilutes the risk by reducing responsibility and, consequently, also motivation, commitment and expectations. Even if the two decision modes were to result in the same level of risk, the risk generated by the impressionistic mode would provide a better basis for action that the risk produced by the rationalistic mode. The rationalistic mode involves much decision rationality and little action rationality; with the impressionistic mode it is the other way round.

3.4   IMPLICATIONS—MANAGING UNCERTAINTY

In this chapter it has been argued that uncertainty is not an automatic effect of particular conditions in the environment or in particular personalities. From a management point of view this is an optimistic conclusion. It appears to be possible to influence the propensity to experience uncertainty and risk, and thus the ability to undertake change actions in given situations and with a given group of people, despite the great potential of these actions for producing uncertainty. The 'unpredictability' of change does not necessarily imply any severe hindrance to change action.

The tendency to perceive change as risky can be modified in two ways, by reducing stakes or by reducing uncertainty. Reducing stakes has the advantage that actions should not be designed in such a way that the effects will be disastrous if they do not succeed. Piecemeal changes are often easier (and safer) to accomplish than revolutions. But if the effects of failure are not going to be disastrous, then a strategy of stake reduction seems an awkward method.

When one decision-maker avoids personal responsibility the risk carried by others will increase, thereby reducing the capacity of the organization as a whole to make decisions with high risk potential. It is therefore better to reduce the stakes on a collective basis. But both personal and collective evasion of responsibility will reduce commitment and dull expectations. When the risk potential is high, firm commitment is often too crucial to allow a strategy of stake reduction. A much better strategy seems to be to reduce the uncertainty component of the risk — by using impressionistic decision modes.

It is possible to provide working conditions favourable to the use of more impressionistic decision modes. If people are expected to consider actions involving a great deal of change, they should not be required to report all the pros and cons that they may have considered or to explain exactly how their decision might affect abstract goals such as profitability, and so on. They should even be protected from people who might regard the project from some other and possibly hostile point of view. The creation of organizational ideologies, which will be discussed in Chapter 5, can help to provide a working environment of this kind. Appropriate evaluation and reward systems can also play a part here: people should be evaluated not by procedures but by results, and it should not be possible to justify failure by claiming that the decision was rationally made. People should be judged by more general criteria than the results of single actions: isolated mistakes should not inspire criticism or provoke punishment.

Preventing risk-taking

Similar arguments can of course also be used in the opposite case, i.e. when the aim is to restrain an organization from action which could be regarded as risky. Here, factors which help people to recognize the uncertainty are those that should be supported. This is the problem that Janis (1972) addresses in his discussion of 'group think' and ways of avoiding it. 'Group think' leads to irrational decisions, with the result that actions carrying too high a risk are undertaken. According to Janis such irrationalities would be avoided if the advantages and disadvantages of actions were carefully investigated, and the impact of other people's actions was not underestimated. Janis observed 'group think' in decisions with extremely high stakes, which suggests that simply increasing the stakes is not an effective strategy, at least not by itself.

Janis' study provokes an interesting reflection: why did the political decision-makers studied make such risky decisions, although the resulting failures would have seemed almost inevitable to an external observer? In light of our discussion above, we could argue that a certain degree of 'group think' in the form of resistance to the perception of uncertainty is a necessary part of an organization if it is to have any power to act. Failures are then inevitable. Rather than always trying to avoid 'group think', we should try to strike a balance between two mistakes: one, being excessively prone to perceive uncertainty, and the other not being prone enough.

Conclusions

After looking more closely at the concepts of uncertainty and responsibility we have been led to question some common conceptions of rationality. If decisions are to be used for the successful initiation of potentially very risky change actions, they have to be reached in a way which researchers producing normative models of decision-making would call irrational. This is not simply a coincidence; it is a logical consequence of the assumptions underlying the rational model. When the outcomes of action are difficult to predict, then action must presuppose some irrationality. Our discussion has also emphasized the difference between making decisions and taking action. Action requires commitment, motivation and expectations, all of which are much influenced by the way the decision is made. Any decision-making which is meant to provide a basis for action should if possible enhance or at least not counteract motivation, commitment and expectations. There is a difference between rational decision-making and good management. Able management researchers do not always make able managers.

Chapter 4

Action Rationalization —Injecting Action Rationality into Rationalistic Decision Processes

I N THE LAST CHAPTER IT WAS ARGUED THAT RATIONALISTIC
decision procedures tend to provide a poor basis for the
kind of organizational actions likely to cause uncertainty,
and that change actions tend to be of just this sort. Rationalistic
decision processes are useful for the purpose of choice but they
are poor initiators of action. But is it not possible to adapt
rationalistic decision processes to support the cause of action?
Two types of organization at least might be interested in an
answer to this question. First, organizations whose ideologies
are inconclusive or inconsistent, can hardly use their ideologies
as instruments of choice. They have to solve their choice
problems before each individual action, and rationalistic
decision processes then provide a tempting solution. Secondly,
in some organizations rationality is prized very highly, and
it is generally assumed that action should be preceded by
rationalistic decision processes. The rationalistic approach may
represent a basis for legitimizing actions and even the
organization as whole. But how can organizations like these
create motivation, and commitment and expectations strong
enough to mobilize organizational action?

In this chapter the dilemma of the simultaneous quest for
decision rationality and action rationality will be illustrated
by the case of a decision process which preceded an
organizational change action. The decision process appeared
to follow the rationalistic mode, but it was adapted to the cause
of organizational action. The case will also serve as an
illustration of our three conditions of action.

The case concerns the restructuring of the Swedish steel
industry within the framework of the Swedish Steel
Corporation, a 50 per cent state-owned company which
answers for over 90 per cent of Sweden's production of
ordinary steel. The restructuring meant that certain parts of
production had to be relocated and this involved serious

61

problems particularly for the many employees who did not want to move. The whole project represented a very difficult organizational action geared to change, and it had to be undertaken in a brand new company incorporating several inconsistent ideologies. The action was preceded by a long and elaborate decision process. The general features of this are described in the following pages.

4.1 A DECISION PROCESS IN OUTLINE

Background

In 1975 the world steel industry was experiencing a deep depression characterized by excess capacity, low prices and deteriorating profitability. The depression had particularly severe consequences for the steel industry in Western Europe, which generally had higher production costs for crude steel than new steel industries in the Third World. In Sweden there were three major producers of ordinary steel at this time. One was the state-owned NJA, situated in Luleå in the north of Sweden on the coast of the Gulf of Bothnia. The others, both privately owned, were Oxelösund in the town of the same name on the Baltic coast in southern Sweden, and Domnarvet in Borlänge some 400 kilometers north-west of Oxelösund, a long way from the coast but close to several old iron-ore fields. NJA and Oxelösund began to suffer heavy losses, which brought Oxelösund to the edge of bankruptcy. Profitability also fell dramatically. At the same time the government and the state-owned NJA were still jointly planning to realize a previous long-term scheme, namely to build a new steelworks in Luleå which would substantially increase Sweden's total capacity for the production of crude steel.

In this situation a government commission was set up to investigate whether the Swedish steel industry could be restructured to become more competitive, and if so how. The commission was to consider the profitability of individual companies, as well as the effects on employment and other factors of the industry's future development.

The commission published its report in March 1977. Its proposals were based on an analysis of ways in which the industry could achieve profitability. Employment problems were not to be allowed to restrict the profitability goal, since permanent subsidies to the steel industry were not considered desirable or acceptable to the country's foreign trade partners. Sales volume in the mid-eighties was expected to be about half the present production capacity. In order to achieve competitive production costs per ton, a drastic reduction in capacity was considered necessary. Economies of scale were regarded as essential to making the industry competitive. The various companies were to specialize on different products. The most important measure in the restructuring of the industry was to be the concentration of crude steel production from iron ore to Luleå and Oxelösund. These two plants showed no significant cost differences compared with Borlänge, but the Borlänge plant was less modern and would require additional investment in environment protection. It was also pointed out that the plants in Oxelösund and Luleå, which are situated on the coast, were not dependent on the rather rare and expensive iron ore from southern Sweden.

The commission compared this solution with the alternative of maintaining crude steel production at all three plants. This would require less investment but a larger work-force, and was not considered to be as profitable as the concentration alternative. Calculations were not presented for any other concentration alternatives (for example a reduction of production in Luleå or Oxelösund).

As a result of the commission's report, the three major steel producers and the government started negotiations to arrange a merger and to get resources from the state for the necessary investments. The union representatives were not satisfied with the limited influence they had been able to exert on the commission's deliberations. They wanted the effects on employment to be taken into consideration in the choice of alternatives, and they demanded representation at the negotiations. Their request was granted, and they employed a consultant to work on the problem.

The union representatives from Borlänge were naturally most dissatisfied with the commission's proposal. They argued that the report should not be taken as the basis for the negotiations, claiming that correct calculations would reveal the unprofitableness of discontinuing the production of crude steel in Borlänge. The negotiators decided to carry out further economic and technical studies before coming to a final decision on the future structure of production. But in order to reach an agreement on the merger the negotiators had to estimate the size of the necessary investment which was to be provided by the government, and for this it was necessary to have some idea of the future production structure. The employees' consultant and the provisional top management together outlined a future structure which in all essentials was the same as the commission's proposal. It was stressed that this structure was just an illustrative example without practical implications. It was called the 'forecast'.

At the end of 1977 the negotiations resulted in a merger of the three companies. The new company, the Swedish Steel Corporation (SSAB), had three owners: the state (50 per cent), and the former owners of the plants in Borlänge and Oxelösund (25 per cent each). But the company was completely dependent on the financial backing of the state. It was to be run on a normal commercial basis. It was agreed that the structure of the company, its personnel policy and various other issues were to be decided after negotiations between management and the unions as soon as the new company had come into being. The creation of a new production structure came to be known as Project SSAB 82, referring to the year by which the new structure was to be realized. The decision process thus generated will be described in further detail below.

SSAB 82

The decision process connected with SSAB 82 started in January 1978. The decision-makers were union representatives from the various plants and top management, and they were involved in the decision process for more than five months on an almost full-time basis. They were served by a vast number of experts. This enormous effort was motivated by the need to make a comprehensive analysis of the relevant issues, to achieve a high level of acceptance for future proposals, to guarantee union influence, and to allow as many people as possible to participate in the decisions.

The written guidelines included a specification that no significant exports outside the Scandinavian countries should be envisaged for the future, but that products should maintain a quality compatible with imported products from other parts of Western Europe.

The first task was to estimate the volume of future sales. Forecasts indicated that crude steel production would be about half existing capacity.

Once agreement had been reached on sales volume, the size and distribution of production capacity were to be determined. The primary alternative was the one proposed by the 'forecast'. This was now compared with an alternative proposal put forward by the unions at Borlänge, whereby the present structure and capacity were to be retained. This alternative was called the 'reference alternative'. Seven variants of the forecast alternative were proposed, but were dropped. Most of the discussions were concerned with ways of calculating costs and prices. The two main alternatives were subjected to economic calculations. At first the results showed no significant differences between the two, even though the Borlänge alternative would mean retaining more excess capacity. The results astonished all parties, and led to renewed estimates of ore prices. New calculations now showed the forecast alternative to be more profitable but the difference was still very small; it could even be argued that it was not significant in view of the many uncertainties involved. The advocates of the forecast alternative then shifted ground: Borlänge was not on the coast and would thus be too dependent on domestic ore, and its plant was not as modern as the others. These facts were already known, of course, and did not call for any complicated calculations.

The last calculations were not completed until a few weeks before the final decision had to be made. Top management and the union representatives from Luleå and Oxelösund still supported the forecast alternative, while the union representatives from Borlänge favoured the reference alternative. Two days before the final decision, the union representatives met to co-ordinate their views. The meeting lasted two whole days and resulted in a compromise whereby the forecast alternative received the support of all the unions, but only on condition that the 'employment situation in the towns concerned should not be allowed to deteriorate'. The compromise was reached after attendance on the Minister of Industry whose answers had been interpreted by the unions as a promise of special government measures to save the employment situation.

While these events were taking place, some external consultants were studying the possible effects of various restructuring alternatives on external factors such as employment and city finances. The results of this study were presented just before the final decision, but were not used by the decision-makers as arguments in favour of any particular alternative. Instead they were used to convince the Minister of Industry of the importance of the unemployment problem.

After the decision

After the decision was made it soon became clear that the decision-makers did not altogether agree on its interpretation. Union representatives from Borlänge held demonstrations in favour of retaining crude steel production there, and this united the union representatives from the other towns in their efforts to keep the plan unchanged. The government set up a new commission to try to transfer other jobs into the Borlänge region. Its subsequent report led to new conflicts, since people in Borlänge found the proposed actions inadequate, and claimed that their condition for acceptance of the re- structuring plan were not being met. However, after some debate they once more had to accept the restructuring plan, but the unions decided to demand an even greater financial contribution from the government in order to provide more jobs.

4.2 A RATIONALISTIC DECISION PROCESS GEN- ERATING COMMITMENT RATHER THAN CHOICE

Two major results emerged from the extensive decision process. One was that the structure of steel production was to remain essentially the same as proposed by the government commission in March 1977. The second was that the new structure began to be implemented. But several questions can be asked regarding the foregoing description of events. Considering all the effort that was put into investigating the profitability of the various alternatives, why did the decision-makers choose the alternative that their own analyses showed to be less profitable? Why did they bother with all those complicated calculations, when the criteria finally used required no such analyses at all? Why was information about external effects called for, and then ignored in the calculations? How did it come about that the decision process resulted in the same recommendation as that made by the government commission, despite the detailed analyses and the participation of the unions? And how was it possible to get all the unions to agree in the end, despite their diverging interests?

No choice

All these questions have one point in common: they presuppose that the decision process dealt with a choice. The decision process was described and legitimized by the decision-makers as a procedure intended to determine the choice between several possible actions. It was also designed in a way that was roughly and superficially consistent with the ideal of decision rationality. But this interpretation of the process as a way of actually dealing with choice, renders it inexplicable. The choice was made independently of the decision process and before the process even started. The decision process contained much more action rationality than decision rationality, but it did not generate all the three conditions of action. Its main function was to generate commitment, as will be explained below.

No generation of motivation or expectations

The three conditions of action were established on quite separate occasions. Motivation was partly established long before the decision process SSAB 82, and partly long after that process was completed. And expectations were established well in advance of SSAB 82. That motivation is established at an early stage is not, of course, unusual. In this case the people representing future top management and most of the unions agreed that, given the circumstances, the main principles of the first alternative presented by the government commission would provide the best solution possible. For Oxelösund, for instance, the proposal was extremely favourable compared with the threat of bankruptcy. Top management and the union representatives from Oxelösund and Luleå favoured the commission's solution throughout the remainder of the process.

On the other hand, the union representatives from the Borlänge plant were not willing to support the solution proposed by the commission. Their favoured alternative, namely not to change the structure, would probably mean that their plant would survive, and that employment would hardly be affected at all.

In other words, it was clear right from the beginning that different decision-makers had distinct and diverging preferences. The likelihood that a rational analysis would determine the choice was slight. On the other hand, it would be equally misleading to describe the process as one of negotiation. The bias towards one solution was clear and strong from the start.

Although no formal decisions had been made before SSAB 82, the parties' expectations regarding the general structure that would be chosen and realized were already formed before the decision process began. It was expected that the 'forecast' proposed by the government commission and the pro-merger group would be implemented. Even most of the representatives from Borlänge who opposed the forecast were certain that it would be put into effect. The decision taken in May embodied expectations that almost all the decision-makers had nursed in January. The decision process had very little impact indeed on the creation of expectations.

This helps to explain several aspects of the process. The only alternative to be considered in any real detail was to maintain present production capacity at all three plants. This alternative was regarded as a 'reference alternative', and as we have seen was actually referred to as such; it was used for comparison with the 'forecast', in order to demonstrate the advantages that the forecast would imply. The idea of a reference alternative explains why an alternative involving no basic structural changes was considered, after all the tedious work of merging the companies. If the aim had been to find another possible structure for production, it would have been more natural to consider alternatives that involved restructuring.

Because expectations were already fixed, the process that ensued was one of argumentation rather than analysis. Whatever the original criteria for accepting the forecast and expecting its realization, the arguments in favour of this solution shifted as the various studies produced new facts.

Both management and unions were astonished when the reference alternative threatened to prove more profitable than the forecast and they found two ways of handling the new information: they changed data used in the calculations, and they shifted ground in their arguments. The price of ore was changed in the calculations, and the 'short-run' profitability for the company suddenly became less important than the need for change and the location and age of the plants. All this made the forecast appear better. New data neither changed the expectations nor the motivation of any of the decision-makers. Instead the decision-makers realized that new data could cause serious disturbances, which is one reason why the study of external effects received scant attention. The main reason for initiating this study was the unions' demand for a broader analysis than the one produced by the government commission. It gradually became clear that the investigation would not produce any arguments in favour of the plan. But as the problematic situation of the Borlänge iron ore mines assumed an increasingly central role in the discussions, it also began to seem likely that an analysis of external effects would militate against the forecast. Thus the only use that was made of this study was as an argument in squeezing more resources out of the Minister of Industry. Consequently the demonstration of severe unemployment problems resulting from the plan did not change the decision; instead it meant that yet another important actor became committed to it.

The decision-makers accepted that the results of the study of external effects and the final calculations would both appear a mere few days before the date scheduled for a decision. This shows once again how little the process had to do with choice; but it also shows the meagre impact of the study on the formation of motivation and expectations.

Naturally, expectations about the structure that would actually emerge greatly affected the outcome. The starting-point for the discussions in the spring of 1978 was in fact the structure proposed by the government commission for realization in 1982 and used as the 'forecast'. The point of departure was not the current situation, as might have been expected. The advocates of a structure more closely resembling the current one but differing from the proposal, were the ones who were regarded as deviants; they were the ones who had to explain themselves and prove their claims. The advocates of the proposal were in a much stronger position, although they were thus supporting drastic changes in the present structure. A revolutionary's dream! Prior investigations had evoked a picture of the future that was far more powerful than the peoples' perceptions of the current situation.

Generating commitment

Thus the situation immediately before the decision process started was such that both motivation and expectations were already fixed, but commitment to the restructuring plan on the part of those involved had still not been declared. Commitment was important to the realization of the plan, the part of those involved had still not been produced. Commitment was important to the realization of the plan, to the actual performance of the organization action. Commitment had been actively avoided at an earlier stage, when the parties rejected previous studies as unacceptable or as being mere calculations with no practical implications. So determined. Only when the process is viewed as a commitment process can it be completely understood.

The parties themselves were fully aware of the function of the decision process. A clear majority described its purpose as being to 'anchor' the forecast/plan in the organization. This even applied to most of the Borlänge representatives, who opposed the plan.

Several methods were used to engender commitment. The most common and most important method, of course, was to include all the parties concerned in the decision-making process and in the final decision. An important function of the formal decision was to commit the decision-makers to it, by sharing responsibility for it among them.

Another way of creating commitment was to gather arguments in favour of the plan. The more similar the basic view to that of the earlier studies, the more easily could arguments be found. Thus profitability arguments and demand forecasts recalling those of the earlier investigations were important. As we have seen, the calculations were made so as to produce arguments favouring the forecast alternative. The other alternative considered was of such a kind that most people hoped it would serve to enhance the picture of the forecast plan. No data which might have been used in argument against the plan, such as the study of external effects, was ever seriously considered. Data of this kind could of course have been used by the opponents from Borlänge, but it would not have had any effect on motivation or expectations. Moreover, at that point the Borlänge party was planning to use much more powerful techniques for avoiding commitment, such as registering certain reservations to the plan. And then by the last two days, when they decided not to enter any reservations, it was too late to avoid commitment by using arguments against the plan. Instead, the fact that a study of external effects had been made somewhat eroded the basis for any future evasion of commitment by reference to external effects — a method that had been tried prior to SSAB 82.

When different preferences are involved, one way of increasing commitment is to make compromise decisions. The various parties carefully watch over 'their' part of the compromise solution, and any change in one part leads to demands for change in others, which makes any alteration in the *content* of the decision a complicated business to be avoided if possible. But the formulation of the compromise also generates commitment, since it gives all parties the impression that they have influenced and participated in the decision.

The commitment effect of compromise explains the great efforts to establish a compromise that were made in the present case, when in fact there had been a majority in favour of the plan decided all the time. Since the content of the decision was determined before the process began, compromise could not be achieved by adapting the content, i.e. by making a choice. From a commitment point of view, what had to be established was the appearance of a compromise, and this was the purpose of the two-day negotiations between the union representatives. Two ways of establishing a compromise were used. First, the decision was formulated so vaguely that different parties could interpret it in different ways. Second, an external party, the Minister of Industry, became committed to the decision. This last had the dual effect of facilitating acceptance of the compromise formulation, and increasing the number of committed parties.

The function of the formal decision-making process was to generate commitment, but the process did not altogether fulfil its role in this respect. The commitment of the Borlänge group was not very strong, as developments during the autumn of 1978 revealed. Different interpretations of the compromise led to several crises in contacts between the unions. It could not be said that the plan was fully accepted until January 1979. But without the decision process Borlänge might have turned the implementation of the plan down in the end.

The decision process may not have resulted in all-out commitment, but it did at least start a process of successive commitment-creation. As time passed, it became increasingly difficult to advocate any other plan. Even the enforced inactivity of awaiting the results of the new commission set up by the Minister of Industry, served to tie people to the plan regardless of their wishes. Since commitment is a social phenomenon, individuals cannot fully control their own commitment, and the Borlänge representatives seem to have lost almost all control over events as the commitment process advanced piecemeal; each step was so small that it was difficult to stop it, and yet it led on almost irresistibly to the next.

Committed representatives

Up to now I have been discussing the commitment of the various representatives. But what about the commitment of the members whom they were representing? The representatives became committed to an action of which they basically disapproved by participating in the decision process. The members had the same view of things, but they did not participate. A discrepancy in the commitment of the two groups could be expected and thus too, a difference in motivation.

However, the representatives do not seem to have been troubled by different views on the part of their members. On the contrary, they were able to exploit them. During the decision process the Borlänge representatives often declared that they must 'go home' for instructions from their members. This was a way of committing the members of the actions of their representatives — a commitment that was important to the representatives, since they knew they were going to 'lose'. At the same time, reference to their members provided the representatives with a way of not committing themselves. They claimed, for example, that their members could not or would not accept particular proposals, although the representatives themselves would like to do so. These tactics were a threat to the very meaning of the process, and the other representatives found them much more disturbing than arguments in the shape of new data or calculations.

Instead, the Borlänge representatives were able to inspire their members to demonstrate against the plan after the May decision. No representative expected the demonstrations to make any difference to the plan itself; rather the idea was to get more resources out of the government and, paradoxically, to create a feeling of unity and support in the unions. This tactic might seem a dangerous one, as anger could have fallen on the representatives later, when the plan was finally accepted. But the representatives assumed that most union members firmly expected the plan to materialize, so that among the union members only a tiny fraction of the demonstrators could possibly have expected their demands to be met.

In another respect the declarations and demonstrations of the union representatives and members in Borlänge served to strengthen commitment to the decision. Many members of the other unions seem to have regarded these actions as a threat to the smooth realization of the whole plan, and so they reinforced their efforts to ensure the execution of something which they had previously disapproved of.

4.3   GENERATING EXPECTATIONS

The firm expectation that a specific action was finally going to be taken helps to explain why the decision process could concentrate on commitment creation. How did these firm expectations arise before the decision process even started? The main explanations can be found in the process of expectation-formulation and in the roles of the opponents to the plan.

The work of the government commission had three important attributes: it was rapid, it concentrated more on formulating a proposal than on analysis, and it did not stress previous acceptance by the groups affected. This meant that the commission could come up with a solution to the problems at about the same time that many of the future decision-makers were beginning to realize just how serious the problems were. It is worth remembering that one of the purposes of the commission was to investigate the effects of a substantial *increase* in crude steel production in Luleå, although this directive was later abandoned. In the public debate and in the minds of many decision-makers the problems and a specific solution became closely intertwined. For some of those involved, the solution itself was really the problem: it was the plans for restructuring the industry that provoked action on the part of the unions. So long as the problems could be tackled by management or state aid, their role was much less important.

Not only the future decision-makers but also members of the local communities and regional planners started contributing to the firm belief that the plan would be realized. Before SSAB 82 this expectation was very strong in the Borlänge region, which substantially reduced the support in the region for the union representatives opposing the plan, and thus in turn reinforced the representatives' own expectations of a similar outcome.

Since the government commission did not seek acceptance for its proposal from the groups affected, the proposal was never perceived as the final decision. Paradoxically this increased its impact on people's expectations. It was not necessary to act immediately, it was better to wait for the 'real' decision. The longer this waiting lasted, the stronger people's expectations became. They gradually accustomed themselves to the proposal. The forecast study had the same effect. Here, too, it was claimed that the investigation was not a commitment, but merely a hypothetical calculation. Expressed in the terms we are using here, it was being claimed that only activities implying commitment were important to the final

decision and to the action itself; activities that roused
expectations were not supposed to be important.

By separating the expectation process from the commitment
process, it was easier to create expectations of negative future
changes. Opponents of the plans were calmed by assurances
that no 'decision' had been made or would be made without
their participation. The protests nevertheless registered by the
opponents had little effect on anyone else for the same reason:
they were to be dealt with later during the 'decision-process'
proper.

4.4 NO INFLUENCE

The decision process was motivated on the grounds that it
would give the unions a chance to exert influence. By
participating in a choice process, they would be able to
influence the decision reached, which would thus be guided
by other motives than profitability. But in the event no such
influence could be observed, mainly of course because the
decision process was not a choice process. Instead the unions'
chances of influencing SSAB 82 lay in their ability to obstruct
the creation of motivation, expectations and commitment to
the proposed plan. But even that kind of influence was difficult
to exert on a basis of the roles and ideologies of the unions.

The unions' traditional role in Sweden resembles that of
the opposition party in a political assembly. They are supposed
to argue against the proposals of the majority but their
arguments are not likely to be accepted. Alternatives do not
even have to be viable or realistic — their function is rather
to express a different will. In this perspective, it is natural
that the SSAB unions' opposition had little influence on their
own or other people's expectations of what would happen.
Later the unions were given a majority role; they were told

that they could actually influence the decision. A sudden complete shift from an oppositional to a majority role was not possible, however, since the unions had to reiterate the old claims from their period in opposition. Thus the altered status of the unions did little to influence expectations. Rather, the participation of the unions gave them 'realistic expectations', as one decision-maker put it. False or over-optimistic hopes could be avoided. Those taking part in the decision process learned to regard the issue from a certain analytical perspective, the same as applied by earlier investigators. This tended to lead to the same results and thus to reinforce prevailing expectations.

The role played by the union representatives was similar to the role of politicians in another respect as well. The representatives formed a group which was itself unable to investigate all the complicated problems which had to be dealt with. They had neither the time nor the necessary expertise. Instead the investigation and problem-solving activities were delegated to experts, who received their directives from the group and submitted their solutions to it. The resources available to the experts in terms of people, time and knowledge far exceeded those of the representatives. The representatives could only inspect the solutions submitted by the experts, without being able to propose any alternatives themselves. Their role could be described as that of a 'defensive inspector' (Brunsson and Jönsson, 1979).

This role is likely to arouse commitment but it is not a good basis for influence: it tends to give decision-makers considerable responsibility for decisions over which they have had little control. Defensive inspectors exert influence essentially by trying to impose their own views on the investigating experts and by trying to achieve marginal adjustments in the solutions presented. The opportunities for influence are further reduced if the inspectors represent different interests. SSAB 82 is a clear case in point.

The first question which the representatives asked about any proposed solution concerned the location of the plant under consideration. All solutions that did not reduce employment in one's own location were accepted, as otherwise something 'worse' might be suggested. At the same time the representatives were unable to say where the different plants should *not* be located as this would have meant openly opposing the unions representing other locations and bringing the inter-union conflict out into the open. Consequently it was always possible to get a majority (two out of three unions) for almost any location plan, regardless of who proposed it. The influence exerted by the unions could hardly have been less. The representatives' only chance of questioning the results of the various investigations was to act as experts themselves, which the Borlänge representatives tried to do by carrying out their own studies.

The unions' interest in concealing their own disagreements was an important element in their ideologies. Another was their conception of the function of the decision process. Since they already expected one particular solution, and since they assumed that the purpose of the process was to create commitment, they did not consider the formal problem (finding the best structure) relevant or difficult. Instead, to most of the union decision-makers the main problem was uniting the unions. They believed that if the unions were unable to present a united front against management, then their influence would be nil (!) and any persistent disagreement among them would show them up as ill-prepared to take part in the management of companies in the future. To use the concepts introduced in Chapter 2, we can say that the problem of uniting the union was a crucial part of both the subjective and the perceived ideologies. But the representatives realized that uniting the unions would be impossible on a basis of their partly conflicting subjective ideologies. Consequently the representatives consciously chose quite a different problem perception as the basis for all their discussions, i.e. as their objective ideology. They hoped to achieve unity by applying 'objective' profitability criterion.

The actual formulation of the problem was thus transformed in three stages: the officially stated problem of finding a structural plan acceptable to the unions triggered off what the unions perceived as the real problem, namely uniting the unions, which in turn engendered the idea of achieving profitability. This series of transformations ultimately produced the same formulation of the problem as that used in the government commission's original investigation.

Some of the union representatives even seem to have made a subjective ideology out of the objective profitability goal; they found it exciting to create a profitable structure. The decision process had also affected motivation. In interviews held after the decision process, no union representative expressed much astonishment of seeing the unions and management striving for the same goals. The unions' main interest was employment. But the problem here was to create conditions for future employment, and for that purpose employment cuts had to be accepted. To a direct question about the influence of the unions, most interviewees seemed surprised and declared that they found the concept of influence irrelevant. When asked to explain themselves, they argued that this had been a decision based on facts, and what does influence mean in such a situation? The management and union perspectives were and should be the same. People who were active both as the unions' and management experts saw no conflict between their two roles.

The ideological inconsistencies complicated the discussions held among the union representatives. There were inconsistencies between the subjective and perceived ideologies and the objective ideologies. Some aspects of the subjective ideologies could not be mentioned at all in the discussions — for example the efforts to create commitment, or the favouring of employment at the representatives' own plant — although almost everybody knew of their existence. Instead arguments could be based on two objective ideologies which in fact were inconsistent, namely influence and profitability. In their search for arguments geared to the profitability goal, the union's representatives had to depend on experts over whom they had no control. All this made their discussions rather confusing. People were forced to use any arguments they could find which favoured their particular interest. Inconsistencies in the argumentation were frequent. Anybody could rightly accuse anybody else of failing to be frank and honest. All this provided fertile soil for serious conflicts, and people were often heard complaining that a personal tone was creeping into the discussions. Coalitions were suspected on all sides. Many decision-makers used the conflicts as an argument for putting an end to the talk and getting down to a decision as soon as possible. It was felt that any more discussion could be irreparable damage to further co-operation. Some of the representatives interviewed declared: 'The result would have been the same if top management had not been there, and the unions had decided for themselves'. This may sound as though the unions were wielding complete and perfect influence. The analysis reveals that the opposite was the case.

4.5 CONCLUSIONS

The organization described in this case embraced several inconsistent ideologies. The organization faced a problem of choice as well as a problem of mobilizing action. Its diverse ideologies favoured different action alternatives: no action could expect strong support from more than one of the ideologies. The striving for influence attested to a wish that no one ideology should completely determine either choice or action.

Action rationalization

The organization tried to solve its problem by means of an apparently rationalistic decision process adapted to the purpose of mobilizing action. Such adaptations of decision processes, which help to transform decision rationality into action rationality, will be referred to here as *action rationalization*. In SSAB 82 four techniques for action rationalization were used: a 'reference alternative' was introduced, data were adapted to decisions, objectives were adapted to data, and the creation of motivation and expectations was separated from the decision process.

The decision process was legitimized by the illusion that it was concerned with a choice. It was easier to create this illusion by introducing several alternatives rather than simply discussing one anticipated action. At the same time, in view of the demand for action rationality, it seemed sensible to compare the expected action with an alternative which was obviously not intended to be realized and which was anyway believed to be bad. It was no more than a 'reference alternative', serving as an example for demonstrating the merits of the expected action. When the reference alternative turned out to be better than expected, some of the data (ore prices) were adapted to fit the alternative that was to be approved. In addition, objectives were adapted to the data, for example, plant location was substituted for profitability.

Since rationalistic decision processes provide poor bases for action, one technique of action rationalization is to deprive the processes of their impact on the creation of some of the action conditions (in extreme cases, all of them). These action conditions can then be moulded in a more action-orientated manner. Our present case illustrates the technique of orientating the decision process towards forming commitments only. This has certain advantages in that participation in the decision process and in the formal decision tends in itself to create commitment by placing responsibility on the shoulders of the decision-makers (cf. Chapter 3). If the technique is to be successful, the decision-makers must know what action to commit themselves to, which means that motivation or expectations (preferably both) should be strong and oriented towards the same action. But our case also shows that motivations which are already determined but are oriented towards different actions, do not necessarily inhibit commitment to one of the actions. Since motivation was already determined here, there was little point in trying to convince other decision-makers of the advantages of one's own alternative. This helps to explain why arguments of this kind did not become intense enough to inhibit commitment. But the separation of the expectation and commitment processes also encouraged the creation of expectations. Since the proposals of the government commission did not commit the parties to anything, the parties in turn felt no compulsion to oppose the proposals. The weak opposition then made the proposals appear more credible. Expectation was all the stronger for having come early — in most cases just as the parties were realizing that there was a problem to be solved. They had no chance to enter the lists by arousing any expectation of a solution of their own.

Action inertia

Despite the action rationalization of the decision process the process was not very strong in generating action. Most of the differences in motivation persisted, and few of the decision-makers were strongly committed to the action. Above all, commitment was closely tied to the exact decision reached; at a later stage top management met stiff resistance to some minor modifications in the decision which were necessary as a result of environmental changes. Since commitment was not based on any common ideology, different decision-makers perceived the value of the modifications in different ways. Opponents of these small adjustments argued that even they would upset the agreed compromise; any change would call for a new decision process for the whole plan. The original decision had mobilized action, but it had also created great inertia.

Implications for influence-wielders

This case is instructive for those hoping to wield influence. It is commonly held that influence should be exerted by participation in decision processes—most laws on co-determination in industry are based on this idea. It is then assumed that decision processes involve both choice and commitment. Would-be influence-wielders offer their commitment in exchange for partial control over whatever decision is made. But the SSAB 82 case shows that even apparently rationalistic decision processes are not necessarily concerned with choice. They may well serve to arouse commitment, however, without endowing participants with any influence. Compromises do not necessarily change the content of a decision, but may still succeed in committing participants to the outcome. Even if decision-participants could command their own commitment, perhaps by actively avoiding commitment to a decision they dislike, they would acquire more influence if they also controlled the creation of expectations and motivation. Effective influence strategies should be directed at all three processes.

In the present case, union influence on the decision was further reduced by the ideological transformations through which the decision passed. Influencing ideologies distinct from influencing decision processes is another way of controlling actions. Ideologies provide a basis for choosing actions which in many respects is better than that provided by a decision process. Ideologies and change actions are the topics of the next two chapters.

Chapter 5

Ideologies and Change
Action

DECISION PROCESSES CAN BE REGARDED AS ONE FORM OF organizational thinking. In the last two chapters we have seen how rationalistic decision processes may inhibit organizational actions for change (Chapter 3) and how rationalistic decision processes must be 'derationalized' — the decision rationality eliminated — and 'action rationalized' instead, if change actions are to result (Chapter 4). Another aspect of organizational thinking involves organizational ideologies, i.e. the tendency of people belonging to the same organization to think similarly about the organization and its environment. This chapter will deal with organizational ideologies. Ideologies determine the ability of organizations to act, both directly and indirectly by way of their influence on decision processes. In Chapter 2 it was argued that three aspects of ideologies were important to organizational action: their conclusiveness, their consistency and their complexity. The first section of the present chapter deals with the relationship between ideologies and decision processes, and we shall see how the conclusiveness of ideologies affects decisions and actions. The second section deals with ideological consistencies and inconsistencies and their impact on organizational change.

5.1 THE IMPACT OF IDEOLOGICAL CONCLUSIVENESS

In Chapter 3 we saw how different modes of assessing proposals for change actions had different effects on uncertainty and commitment and, hence, on the ability to change. Two extreme modes of decision-making were described — the rationalistic mode and the impressionistic. The impressionistic mode of decision-making provides a much better preparation for organizational action than the rationalistic mode. On the other hand, an impressionistic approach hardly seems to be a good way of solving the choice problem, of finding out which action is the best. As we found in Chapter 4, it is difficult to prepare for choice *and* mobilization for action in one and the same process. In the present section we will examine the way in which ideologies can be used for solving the problem of choice, thus helping to determine which mode of decision-making can be used. The discussion will be based on an elaboration of the case already presented in Chapter 3. The decision processes described there occurred in two companies which differed not only in their modes of decision-making and their ability to undertake change actions but also in their ideologies.

The two companies belonged to an industry in which innovativeness was important to profitability and survival. Most of the traditional products were exposed to keen competition from foreign producers and had become unprofitable. It was necessary to reorient production towards new areas, by developing new products for fresh markets.

But, as was mentioned in Chapter 3, product development projects represent difficult organizational actions with a high uncertainty potential. Very strong expectations, motivation and commitment are needed. In product development projects which are concerned with mere variations in existing products there is normally less potential uncertainty and successful product development is more easily achieved.

Objective ideologies

In both companies the need for change by way of product development was strongly felt. Both spent a good deal on product development activities. Both were anxious to design 'strategies' or objective ideologies, to use the terms introduced in Chapter 2, for their product development activities, which would indicate the kinds of products that should be developed. These objective ideologies were fairly consistent with the companies' subjective and perceived ideologies. But the ideological structures differed substantially.

In one of the companies the change strategy was to be as permissive as possible. Proposals were not to be restricted in advance, and any proposals were welcome. The ideology consisted almost entirely of normative principles which were broad in scope and fairly vague: new products were to be profitable, they were to require substantial investment and they should involve system solutions rather than details. Any proposal that could be expected to lead to profitable products would be accepted, with a few clearly stated exceptions. It was hoped that this ideology would maximize the chances of accomplishing change.

Profitability was the ultimate goal even in the other company. But apart from this, the ideology of the second company was almost the complete opposite of the one described above. It was very restrictive: only proposals for new products within a narrow and precisely stipulated area were acceptable. This was justified by a complex line of reasoning, which enlarged the descriptive element in the ideology. The market organization was regarded as the solid base of the company, representing the major investment which should be exploited as much as possible. The chosen market was for products in a particular price class for use in a specific industrial sector. Sales of these products were supposed to be very insensitive to price, which made the products highly profitable. This idea was based on a conception of the way in which buying decisions were made in the customer firms. The products were normally sold through wholesale dealers.

The managers also had a clear conception of what motivated the sellers in the wholesale firms. Certain product requirements regarding technical complexity, size, profitability and uniqueness, were thus held to be essential.

As is clear from this short description, the ideology of this company consisted of a multidimensional explanatory model of the market. The model contained elements which were strongly interconnected in terms of cause and effect. How the abstract goal of profitability was to be reached was specified in terms of a hierarchy of elements, of which the lowest were directly operational.

In theoretical terms the ideologies differed in complexity and conclusiveness. One ideology was very simply, containing some normative elements but few descriptive ones and few causal interrelationships. The other was very complex: it contained many elements in a description of reality and many causal interrelations between these elements.

The first ideology contained very broad and ambiguous descriptive and normative elements. Broad elements subsume a large slice of reality, or many possible actions. Ambiguous elements are difficult to use for classifying observations or behaviours; they are vaguely or inoperationally defined. A broad element has wide boundaries, and an ambiguous element has diffuse boundaries. The result is the same; both breadth and ambiguity allow the ideology to cover a wide array of situations and actions. In the broad and ambiguous ideology in our case a few precise specifications of what was *not* acceptable, left an almost infinite number of possible proposals for new products which might be pronounced acceptable. Furthermore, no one really knew what was meant by 'system solutions', or how profitability could be forecast in practice. It was difficult to conclude from the ideology whether or not a proposal ought to be accepted. The other ideology contained much narrower and clearer elements: it was very conclusive, which meant it was easy to assess whether or not a given proposal was consistent with it.

Ideologies and decision-making

As would be expected from the discussion in Chapter 2, the different ideologies were combined with different modes of decision-making. The company with the inconclusive ideology was the one which used the rationalistic mode described in Chapter 3, while the company with the conclusive ideology employed the impressionistic mode. The decision modes are natural consequences of the ideologies. A conclusive ideology has already solved much of the choice problem, and the individual action can be preceded by processes which create commitment and motivation instead of by processes of choice. A non-conclusive ideology leaves a much greater part of the choice problem unsolved, and the organization has to solve this problem before each individual action. A rationalistic decision mode might then be needed, since it is a tool for choice.

This description of the different ideological situations may reassure the reader who felt concerned, after perusing the description in Chapter 3, about how the company with the impressionistic mode chose its new product projects. Now it should be clear that the company transferred most of its choice problem to earlier phases of the product development process prior to the decision process. People in this company did not even suggest projects that were inconsistent with the ideology. And when an idea was proposed by some external source, it was very easy to tell whether or not it should be rejected.

The ideology left little scope for different interpretations or disagreement among the decision-makers. The choice was made by the ideology, not by any decision. But part of the choice function was also transferred to later phases. It was not considered disastrous if a project failed and had to be cancelled after some development work had already been done. In the next chapter it will be shown how this attitude makes sense, as a result of the complex ideology to which the people adhered.

Attribution

The companies' ideologies not only had contrasting structures; even their contents differed. They differed in attribution. The company with the complex and conclusive ideology had very strong self-attribution. An example can illustrate this. It was discovered that there was a product already on the market which was very similar to one proposed in the company. The main feature of both these products was that they were far less noisy than other similar products; the main difference in their design was that they were made of different materials. Furthermore, the sales of the existing product were small. People were asked whether they found this information important in making their own decision. The answer was that they neither knew nor had tried to estimate their competitors' sales. If they had known these figures, they would not have been able to use them in their assessment of the project, because the success of their product depended on their own ability to develop a good product and to market it well. The sales of the competing product were a result of the way the competing firm had designed and marketed their own product. Thus the sales figures did not contain any useful information.

In the other company people instead evinced very strong 'environment attribution': they tended to consider parts of the environment as decisive to the fate of their products.

Competitors, customers and authorities were regarded as being more influential than they were themselves. Their assessment of a product which was completely new to the market illustrates this attitude: the relevant proposal was rejected since some decision-makers thought that the competition would be too keen; other producers would eventually come up with products with the same function but with different technical solutions, and finally one solution would surpass the others and bring very high rewards. But the number of misses would also be high, which meant that there was a high risk of the product proving a failure.

Self-attribution involves a strong sense of personal control. When turned on the assessment of future events, it engenders a planning approach: the future is something that can be planned. The point of planning is to make sure that you know what you want and then to commit yourself to it. This is highly consistent with the outcome of an impressionistic decision mode. Environment attribution accords better with the rationalistic mode. If events are determined by the environment rather than by you, you can try to predict future events and then try to adapt to them. Rationalistic decisions can be regarded as attempts to predict the effects of a considered action on objectives. Effects are estimated, not created.

Ideologies and change

The ideologies of these companies helped to determine which decision modes could be used, thus also affecting the companies' ability to change. By solving the choice problem ideologically, one of the companies could use an impressionistic mode — an approach that gave a low level of uncertainty and a high degree of motivation, commitment and expectation.

This made it easier both to accept and to carry out new product projects. The company was one of the most innovative in the industry; it changed its product mix quickly and enjoyed very high profitability and a high growth rate.

The rationalistic decision mode in the other company led to severe difficulties in accepting and implementing new product projects. The decisions generated too much uncertainty and too little motivation and commitment expectations for most of the new product projects to be possible at all. More resources were spent on minor developments of existing products, where the uncertainty potential was much less. The company's survival was threatened. The strategy of maximum permissiveness in order to accomplish change did not work in practice. It simply meant that the function of choice was brought closer to the actions, which in turn led to rationalistic decisions. The strategy of accepting everything proved to be a mistake.

5.2 SOCIAL DEADLOCK—THE IMPACT OF IDEOLOGICAL INCONSISTENCIES

The structures of ideologies can be described not only in terms of their conclusiveness and complexity but also of their consistency. The two companies in the previous section exemplified highly consistent ideologies. In this section an organization will be described in which the ideologies were highly inconsistent.

Inconsistencies might seem likely to promote change. A variety of conflicting views on the nature of the situation and what should be done about it, should lead to many ideas for change. But inconsistencies obstruct organizational action, which means that on the whole inconsistencies represent a major obstacle to organizational change actions. This can be illustrated by an extreme case, a case in which the ideological inconsistencies were very great and the action outcome a social deadlock.

Social deadlock is the opposite of organizational change. Deadlock occurs when a group of people have arrived at a situation which satisfies none of them but which they are unable to change. Instead their attempts to change things simply serve to reinforce the existing state of affairs. A social deadlock may be full of individual actions aimed at bringing about a change, but the situation as a whole does not alter. It becomes increasingly stable and fossilized.

An organization striving for change

Runtown is a small town in southern Sweden with about 10 000 inhabitants. It was created as the result of a merger of three small towns in 1970. The town has the standard organization of all Swedish municipalities, determined by law. It is ruled by politicians elected for three years. The politicians are organized in a municipal council of 49 members. An executive committee of seven people and a number of other committees are elected by the municipal council at the beginning of each election period. The members of the council and the committees cannot be changed during the election period. The executive and the other committees consist of politicians from all parties of any appreciable size.

Seven parties were represented on the Runtown council. Two of these were socialist parties forming one loose coalition, and three were liberal parties forming another. The other two parties had no traditional ties with either of the coalitions and were very small. Neither the liberal nor the socialist parties had a majority in the council, but the liberal members had a few more seats and therefore held the majority in the executive and in all the committees.

The organization was a political one in which conflicts were institutionalized (Chapter 7). In a political organization ideologies should be inconsistent. But in Runtown the inconsistencies did not only follow party lines. In particular politicians from different parts of the town represented different interests and opinions. The ties between politicians from the same district were often stronger than those between members of the same parties.

The politicians had a staff of managers and officials employed on a basis of their professional merits. These officers were supposed to be objective, politically speaking. Their task was to run the everyday business of the executive, to undertake the investigations needed by the politicians for their political decisions, and finally to put the decisions into effect.

The financial situation of the town was deteriorating throughout the 1970's, and the need for investment was increasing all the time. New schools, a new water supply system and a new sewage system were among the investments that had to be made. New apartments had to be built so that young people would be able to stay in the town instead of moving away as many had been doing.

The executive had previously solved an unemployment crisis by persuading companies to move plants to the town. For a long time the municipal executive tried to solve all new problems by intensive efforts to attract more companies. This policy was not successful, and no new companies arrived. In fact it was becoming increasingly difficult for companies to move in; the lack of investment had led to a shortage of apartments and building sites, and there was a great shortage of skilled workers.

Not only were the external problems difficult to manage. The internal situation was no easier. It was hard to get a majority for any specific action. It was difficult to forecast whether or not an executive proposal would be accepted in the council. The opportunities for planning were very restricted. Distrust and suspicion were widespread. The debates regularly deteriorated into harsh personal attacks. Even quite simple actions such as 'normal' building activities failed to be carried out.

By 1975 the external problems had reached critical proportions. During the summer water had to be supplied by truck to some parts of the town, and the council administration building was condemned by the public health authorities. At the same time the financial position of the town was growing worse than ever. That same year two solutions to the problems were suggested, apart from the traditional one. Neither solution could really solve the most acute problems, but they were intended to have a somewhat long term effect. The idea was to prevent the executive from landing in further crises by introducing new and better forms for the work of the executive committee. One of the proposals was to reorganize the executive, the other was to introduce a system of long-term budgeting.

The attempts to bring about these organizational changes led to a further deterioration in the organizational climate, and in 1976 nearly all the leading municipal officials left their posts and moved away from the town. After this crisis the external situation gradually improved, and the financial conditions became fairly satisfactory. A more realistic view of the employment situation was now accepted and the policy of attracting new companies was abandoned. New municipal officials were employed, and despite great difficulties some building activities started and some decisions were taken on part of the organizational changes previously attempted. Soon, however, the internal situation was growing increasingly tense. The handling of housing policy provides a good example of this.

Housing policy had been a controversial issue ever since the municipal merger in 1970. Before the merger the politicians in the largest district had agreed on a plan for new housing areas. Their decision was not accepted by the new majority in the merged organization. For more than six years alternative plans had been investigated, and a severe shortage of houses and of sites for building had arisen. Discussions had become irritated, and were one of the main reasons for the polarization between politicians from the previously independent districts.

When discussing the housing programme for 1978 to 1982, the opposition in the council claimed that building in one area should start a year earlier than the municipal officials proposed. According to the officials, this was impracticable. A majority on the council then decided that the houses were anyway to be built a year earlier. People were greatly agitated, and in this mood they decided to form a special committee to supervise the executive and to see that the building policy was actually carried out. This was a unique decision with no legal authority. Some politicians appealed against it in the regional court. A series of sessions were then dominated by debates about the supervisory group, about the more exact meaning of the decision, about whether illegal alternations had been made in the minutes after the first session, and so on. The affair was generally regarded as a public scandal by the politicians themselves, by the press, and presumably by most of the townsfolk. All the leading politicians thought that the executive and council had made fools of themselves yet again. The housing programme was further delayed.

The negotiations between the municipality and the regional authorities about the building of a medical care centre provide another example of people desperately trying to get some action. Just before the negotiations were to be terminated, and behind the executive's back, some leading politicians got in touch with representatives from the regional authority and showed them an alternative building, which would be better for the regional authority but more expensive for the town. After that there was no hope of the original building being approved and the municipality had to accept the alternative. Everyone agreed that it was wrong in principle to side-step the executive, but those who had done it claimed that it was the only way of 'getting anything done'! Needless to say, this episode did nothing to improve the internal social situation.

Owing to events like this, the mood in the municipality by the early summer of 1978 had reached rock-bottom. The coalition parties had lost most of their confidence in one another. The members of the county council appeared to feel deep mistrust for the municipality. Suggestions in the council to alter or shelve the executive's proposals were always greeted with applause. Decisions were often extremely difficult or almost impossible to put into practice in the way planned by the county council. The municipality also had difficulty in implementing their decisions at all. Often decisions were simply not carried out, or were delayed in committees, and so on. Most of the people concerned spoke of action being 'paralysed'. And this paralysis was of course bad for the town's development. The situation also released a good deal of strong aggression among people. They accused each other of wanting to create problems. The tone between the politicians was sharp, and the atmosphere bad. Rumours were rife that one party or other had conspired against other parties and against the best interests of the local community. The politicians formed 'opinion' groups, centred mainly on issues rather than party lines. One of the liberal parties was more often in agreement with opposition parties than with the other liberals. The politicians from the main population centre often found themselves opposing the politicians from other parts of the municipality, regardless of their party affiliations. People voted inconsistently in different committees and at different meetings; one person might vote for a proposal in a committee and against it in the council.

External parties were in an increasingly strong position. The county council benefited from the conflict between the politicians about the medical centre. Business firms gained influence by way of the demands they made. The demands were supported by many people — many of them who played the role of opponents to the chairman, the majority of the Runtown politicians and administration in general used the company demands as arguments. The municipal officials, who did display less conflict than the politicians, gained more and more influence. This gave more influence to the municipal officials as well. After a year or so they succeeded in starting the erection of a new office building.

All the main parties agreed that the prevailing situation was very dangerous and uncomfortable. Most of their thoughts and feelings were occupied by these problems, and they felt confused and frustrated. Everyone considered that the municipality was inadequately controlled. Concrete actions failed to materialize or were wrong, and the town was acquiring a bad reputation. Many people even found it difficult to explain their own actions, and admitted that they were inappropriate. And yet people continued to act in the same manner, so that the conflicts simply grew and the situation deteriorated.

People tried to get some organizational action by bypassing the municipal officials, for example, or by continually voicing their mistrust of the council or the executive committee. But this behaviour only aggravated the problems and reinforced the stalemate. Most people finally concluded that some people, including themselves, would have to be replaced before the crisis could be solved.

A pattern had developed among the parties resulting in a situation which no one desired but from which no one could withdraw. Instead the situation misled people to act in a way which only aggravated the crisis. This is just what characterizes a social deadlock. The deadlock not only prevented change; it also inhibited almost all kinds of organizational action. In the following pages the deadlock will be explained in light of the organizational ideologies of Runtown.

Organizational ideologies in Runtown

The organizational ideologies in Runtown go a long way towards explaining the origins and persistence of the social deadlock. Ideological inconsistencies in particular were crucial. Before describing these inconsistencies, we should look a little more closely at the concept of organizational ideology.

In Chapter 2 three kinds of organizational ideology were distinguished. The subjective ideology is the sum of the members' individual cognitive structures. Perceived ideology is what organization members think that their fellow members think. An objective ideology consists of ideas shared (but not necessarily believed), by the members, which are used in discussion and taken as arguments for action. The content of ideologies will be described in two dimensions. Ideologies can refer to how things are (have been or will be) and to how things should be. The first aspect is descriptive and the second normative. Both aspects can contain answers to a number of questions (Table 5.1).

Table 5.1   The content of organizational ideologies

| Question | Aspect | |
	Descriptive (is)	Normative (should be)
How	Routine	Procedure
What	Ontology	Objective
Why	Attribution	Goals

A first question is 'How?' The facets of the ideology which answer this question will describe or prescribe how members act or should act in relation to one another or to people outside the organization. The descriptive aspect of the answer (how things are) will be referred to as *routine*, and the normative aspect (how things should be) as *procedure*.

A second question is 'What?' This refers to the organization, its environment and the situation. What matters here is not only what people perceive as the facts; which facts are considered important and which are not is also interesting. What has been, and what will be, is also part of the ideology. The descriptive answer to the 'what' question is referred to as *ontology*, and the normative answer as *objective*.

Thirdly, ideologies can answer the question '*Why?*' The descriptive aspect here is refered to as *attribution*. An important distinction has proved to be the extent to which causes are to be found in the individual, in the organization, or in the environment. The normative aspect refers to what or who should control the situation and can be termed goals.

The contents of the ideologies in Runtown can now be described. The *subjective* ideology will be described first.

Procedure and routine. Awareness of how matters should be handled in municipal administrations in general and in Runtown in particular, was strong in all the people concerned. Procedure and routine were very important to them. Existing ideas can be summarized in the following list. Common to them all is the view that the politicians should discuss and decide on municipal actions on a basis of their different values.

(1) Differences of opinion should be based on ideological and political loyalties.
(2) Conflict should be between parties and not between people or groups within the parties.
(3) There should not be alliances between the liberal and the socialist parties.
(4) The duty of the opposition is to criticize the majority.
(5) The politicians should agree on the problems; conducting 'politics' has no value in itself

(6) Discussions should be factual, not 'political'.

(7) Opinions should be aired and agreements made openly in the local government or local council when the relevant matters are raised.

Many of these ideas are internally inconsistent, for example (1) and (6), (4) and (6). The ideological inconsistencies were general; it was not a question of certain groups of people possessing different but internally consistent ideologies; there were no 'sub-ideologies', connected with the political parties, the executive or the local council for example. And the cognitive structure of the individual parties were roughly as inconsistent as the ideology: all the people interviewed endorsed at least five of the first six ideas listed above and most of them endorsed all six.

Ideas about how the municipality should act were not particularly well matched by ideas about how it worked in practice: procedure and routine were not consistent. The following were people's ideas about how the organization actually functioned:

(1) There are conflicts with the parties.

(2) There are conflicts based on the area in the municipality in which the people reside.

(3) There are alliances between the liberal and socialist parties.

(4) To a great extent the conflicts are of a 'personal' nature (conflicts between persons instead of conflicts about values and facts).

(5) Conflicts are strong.

(6) Agreement between the parties is negotiated before the questions are raised in the local government or local council.

These ideas, too, were shared by all the people, who thus agreed that existing routines did not coincide with the procedures which they thought should apply. Dissatisfaction with the present situation was also expressed with considerable emotional emphasis.

The sixth idea refers to a condition which most of the actors thought of as 'conspiracy'. Conspiracy was always something engaged in by other people and never by themselves. It represented their main explanation of the awkward fact that the vote in the executive and the council did not always tally. Since no single person admitted taking part in such conspiracies it is possible or even probable that they did not really exist.

Ontology and objective. There were some minor differences in the views of people on the municipality's present and future financial situation. The main difference existed between those who thought that the situation was generally speaking good, and those who thought it was bad. The differences had nothing to do with diverging goals, but originated in different judgement of the facts and different expectations. The optimists generally belonged to the majority parties, while the pessimists belonged to the opposition.

A further difference applied to the perception of individual issues. The municipality people had more detailed knowledge of the issues and were more concerned with the practical problems and their execution. The county councillors did not realize that the execution of their decisions was complicated by serious problems. Nor did they know about the issues in detail.

Even if there were differences of opinion about how individual issues should be handled, there was considerable consensus about what should be striven for.

Attribution and goals. Initially people in Runtown tended to explain the municipality's situation largely in terms of factors in the environment and outside the council's own control. During the deadlock this environment attribution changed character. Many people later explained what had happened by referring only to the municipality's own actions. Usually the chairman of the executive was blamed. Thus, on the individual level, environment attribution was retained. As regards escaping from the deadlock, everyone declared, 'There is nothing *I* can do'. If anyone *was* considered capable of doing anything, it was never the speaker himself. The normative aspect — who *should* control the situation — was not clear, but most people agreed that the chairman should not exert strong control.

The perceived ideology agreed to a certain extent with the subjective ideology; that is to say, in certain respects people had an accurate picture of what other people thought, for instance about how the work in the community administration should be carried out and how it actually was carried out. To a great extent this also applied to ontology and attribution. The major difference between subjective and perceived ideology concerned goals. Those interviewed held that other people (apart from their own inner circle) were primarily interested in strengthening their own power positions and undermining the power of others. This striving for personal power on all sides (except by the speaker) was widely regarded as the real reason for the deadlock.

In general there was a strong tendency among people to assign to each other more insight into what was going on than they possessed themselves. 'I don't understand so much, but the others work consciously for personal power and make agreements with another about the methods.'

The objective ideology in Runtown was provided at an early stage with two principal ideas: 'The problems are considerable, and there is not much we can do about them.' Other problems were then added to the list. It was felt that the most appropriate strategy would be to apply for help from outside, either from the government authorities or by attracting business into the area. This ideology was neither particularly well developed nor particularly suitable as a basis for the solution of the problems. But at least it resulted in a kind of fundamental unanimity and a common basis for discussion.

However, the basis for the objective ideology gradually disappeared. In the long run it became difficult for any individual to argue that he was completely blameless. And the new municipal officials could prove that the situation was not as disastrous as people thought. Gradually people realized that the strategy of attracting business or of appealing to the government authorities was not an appropriate solution to their problems.

No new objective ideology had appeared to replace the old one. Instead, a common picture of reality was simply lost. Now there was not even any starting-point for discussion, and lack of unity was felt even more strongly. The absence of objective ideology also caused problems for the opposition. It is difficult to present an opposing ideology in a vacuum.

Ideologies and social deadlock

The ideologies described above were only too likely to create a persistent social deadlock. And the most serious aspect of the ideologies was their inconsistency. The following is a list of the inconsistencies and their effects.

Inconsistencies in cognitive structures regarding procedure. Ideas about how the work of the municipal administration should be done were internally inconsistent. Consequently it was impossible to establish a work routine which fulfilled all demands. The parties were doomed to dissatisfaction with whatever routine they had, and to frustration because they could not see any solution. All routines could be criticized, and nobody could repudiate the criticism for being based on false values. This aspect of the ideology also had the direct effect, which is intrinsic to cases of social deadlock, that the parties were dissatisfied with their present situation but could not think of a better alternative.

Inconsistencies between descriptive and normative aspects. The inconsistencies in ideas of about how the work should be done implied dissatisfaction with the present working system, i.e. inconsistencies between routine and procedure. In addition people thought that the town's situation was not what it ought to be — there were great inconsistencies between ontology and objectives. For many people there was also a major inconsistency between attribution and goals. They blamed the chairman for what happened, but at the same time they did not want him to control things. Inconsistencies between descriptive and normative aspects should not normally lead to paralysis; on the contrary they can sometimes trigger off action. But in Runtown the inconsistencies were too great. The parties tried to solve three problems at the same time: they were trying to change the working system, the situation of the municipality, and the balance of power. This obviously overloaded the organization's problem-solving capacity.

For instance, attempts to improve the financial situation were used to try to change the working system and the balance of power, and vice versa.

Almost every action could be seen as intended to change either the municipality's situation, or the routines, or the power. For example, the reorganization proposal was seen by some people as a procedural issue and by others as primarily a question of cost for the municipal administration in a difficult financial situation. The housing issue became partly a fight about the authority of the county council versus that of the municipality. Thus the arguments came to be based on two entirely different perspectives, and the parties found it difficult to anticipate and understand one another's positions. In particular it was difficult to find a solution which could be accepted in both perspectives, and on which most people could agree.

Inconsistencies in subjective ideology regarding ontology. The parties had different conceptions of the real nature of the situation. This contributed to the deadlock, but an even more important factor was that the differences of opinion depended on the roles which the parties played (e.g. opposition roles and majority roles). They could not just talk themselves into a unanimous conception. In addition, roles were not only distributed according to accepted groupings. Often people holding the same ideas did not form natural groups within the organization (e.g. parties). The structure of the ideology did not correspond to the social structure. The conflicting ideas did not form any clear alternative sub-ideologies tied to subgroups, which people could support or oppose.

. . . *but agreement on goals.* In itself, agreement on the situation that should be striven for should hardly cause a social deadlock. However, within the framework of the ideologies in Runtown the effect was exactly that. Agreement on goals made the disagreements and the conflicts more difficult for people to understand. One element of the subjective ideology was that there could be disagreement about goals. It would have been easier to understand a situation in which the opposition was opposing because it was striving for a different goal. The situation even led people to construct other goals for their opponents (cf. perceived ideology below).

Inconsistencies between subjective ideologies regarding procedure and reality. In their attempts to understand one another's behaviour, people formed opinions of what was going on which, as far as can be judged from outside, did not agree with reality. They believed that the others were conspiring together in various ways, and these misinterpretations tended to gain in strength with time. Looking back, a suspicion of conspiracy was seen as a certainty, and as it was thus 'known' that the opposition had conspired on earlier occasions, then one could be certain that they were doing so now. The conspiracy theory provided a temporary feeling of greater security — here, at least, was *one* explanation to fall back on. In terms of any real understanding of the situation which could lead to a solution it was of course a red herring, serving only to increase the deadlock.

Inconsistencies between subjective and perceived ideologies. In their attempts to understand the situation, the parties attributed goals to each other which they did not have. Like the differences between ideology and reality, the differences between subjective and perceived ideology were the cause of misjudgements which hindered any escape from the social deadlock. (Similar results have been reported by Dale and Spencer, 1977.)

To sum up: inconsistencies were found in cognitive structures about procedures, within the subjective ideology, between the subjective ideology and reality between subjective and perceived ideologies, and between descriptive and normative aspects of the ideologies. Apart from these inconsistencies and the inconsistencies regarding objectives, two other ideological qualities affected the social deadlock.

Environment attribution. Environment attribution is a bad starting-point for any attempt to escape from a social deadlock. In Runtown everyone felt powerless; it was not even worth trying to get rid of the stalemate. And since the scapegoats were to be found in the parties' own organizations, the conflicts simply grew stronger.

Lack of objective ideology. The lack of objective ideology meant that people had no common ideological platform from which they could make common analyses. There was no basis for discussion. This of course reduced the feeling of togetherness and limited the opportunities for starting a dialogue. Even an undeveloped objective ideology can be developed so as to represent a larger part of the subjective ideology, and this might reduce the risk of a deadlock. In the present case, there was no basis for such a development.

The ideologies prevailing in Runtown provided a prime cause of social deadlock and of the difficulties in escaping from the deadlock once it had arisen. Our description of the ideologies shows that the 'confusion' experienced by the parties was certainly understandable, but that the reasons for it went deep. Attempts to understand and eliminate the confusion simply reinforced the deadlock. Instead of understanding, misunderstandings arose, and this made it even more difficult to resolve the stalemate.

Many features of the organizational ideologies brought the need for change home to the parties. Since they anyway disagreed about the nature of the situation in the organization, there was a high probability that at least some of them would perceive a need for change at any time. The inconsistencies in cognitive structures, which meant that opposing values prevailed, made people feel dissatisfied with any present state of affairs, and this is always a strong incentive to change. The inconsistencies between descriptive and normative aspects must also have had this effect. And in fact the ideologies did lead to a series of individual and group actions aimed at achieving change, but the actions did not result in any organizational renewal. The same ideological features that made people perceive the need for changes, prevented any organizational changes from getting under way.

At the individual level inconsistencies in cognitive structures did not provide a strong platform for engendering motivation for any specific action. On the organizational level, these inconsistencies meant that any change action could be criticized on grounds which the parties felt to be as correct as the grounds for making the change. Inconsistencies in subjective ideology made it difficult to form common expectations of what specific changes might occur, and of what would happen to any attempt at achieving a specific change. The same is true of the great inconsistencies between descriptive and normative ideological aspects, which made it difficult to predict whether other people would use an action as a method of changing the working system, the situation or the balance of power. The inconsistencies in ontology made it difficult to build up common motivations for any specific organizational action. Inconsistencies in procedures made it possible to criticize any proposal for new ways of doing things, thereby reducing motivation and commitment.

People tried to find models whereby they could explain and predict the behaviour of others, thus enabling themselves to have expectations about other people's reactions to attempted changes. But the models they constructed were inaccurate since there were marked inconsistencies between subjective and perceived ideologies. This meant that people's expectations were unreliable, and the parties felt uncertain. Besides, the general model was that the parties were trying to block each other's change initiatives.

Instead of strong common expectations and motivation, the ideologies produced confusion and considerable frustration. They made people avoid commitment; not even voting was seen as a real commitment, and the same people could vote in favour of a proposal at one meeting and against it at another. In particular it was impossible to get all the main parties to commit themselves to the same action.

Shared objectives were obviously not sufficient to bring about organizational change. The ideological inconsistencies created a strongly felt need for change, but they obstructed expectations, motivation and commitment in connection with any specific change action, thus impeding any real renewal. Instead of commitment, the ideologies produced conflict.

Conflict

There can be various kinds of conflict. Conflict can spring from opposing interests between two parties, constituting one way (among others) of dealing with the situation. Strikes are a means of urging the interests of one party on the labour market. This kind of conflict is what Coser (1956) called realistic conflict. But there are other conflicts which serve simply as a way of relieving tension among the parties; the conflict is an end in itself and can arise with anyone at all. These are the characteristics of unrealistic conflicts. Real-life conflicts can resemble both these 'ideal types'. A conflict based on diverging interests can also serve to relieve tension, and an unrealistic conflict can lead to perceived differences in interests.

Conflict is important to an understanding of organizational action, since it greatly reduces the likelihood of commitment. Commitment is a major prerequisite of organizational action; conflict is an effective obstacle to such action. A conflict between two parties is a strong expression of their differences, signalling the parties, decision not to co-operate in a common action — it is their 'de-commitment'. In a conflict you expect your adversary to work against you and not with you.

In Runtown, the conflicts between the parties became very severe, representing undeniable obstacles to organizational change. The conflicts were both realistic and unrealistic, and they were intimately related to the ideological inconsistencies and the parties' attribution of blame. They arose in a climate of frustration and confusion. There were several reasons for feeling frustrated, apart from the dissatisfying situation itself. People were uncertain whether they understood what was going on. Inconsistencies in the cognitive structures meant that some of their problems had no solution. Generally speaking a huge gap had developed between the desire to do something and the ability to do it.

The confusion was due to the parties difficulty in understanding each other's behaviour. A tentative reconstruction would put the ideological characteristics in the following order: people experienced several situations in which other people did not behave as expected. They then constructed explanations for this behaviour, in which other people were assigned ideologies and secret ways of behaving other than those they actually had. People did not believe each other's arguments for their actions. Inconsistencies arose between perceived and subjective ideologies and between ideology and reality. Most people assumed that other people's actions were secretly intended to counteract their own, and to make it worse they attributed this to the other people's personalities: they were evil people. Therefore their behaviour could not be changed. This theory about other people was sufficiently general to make almost any counteractive behaviour seem what was 'only to be expected'. Thus the theory was confirmed over and over again.

The conflicts became realistic in the sense that people actually (although incorrectly) attributed interests to their colleagues that differed from those they held themselves. But frustration also rendered the conflicts unrealistic. They were extremely emotional, making people prepared to hurt one another in ways which served neither their own purposes nor the organization's.

It may be recalled that conflict was also a threat to the commitment process in the Swedish steel case (Chapter 4). There, too, ideological inconsistencies were important. There were inconsistencies in the objective ideology, as well as between objective ideology on the one hand and perceived and subjective ideologies on the other. People actually had to be 'dishonest': they had to present arguments which they did not really believe in but which favoured their own interests. This meant that obviously realistic conflicts acquired an unrealistic element as well. The union representatives began to feel hostile towards one another. But these conflicts arose after commitment had been largely achieved. In both SSAB and Runtown inconsistencies between subjective, perceived and objective ideologies created conflicts which impeded or threatened organizational action.

5.3 CONCLUSIONS

To sum up, so far the argument has led to the following conclusions. Organizational ideologies affect expectations and motivations in organizations. If ideologies are conclusive and consistent enough, they tend to lead organization members to expect the same actions and to feel motivated for them. Organizations with conclusive and consistent ideologies do not have to engage in choice procedures before each action. Expectations, motivation and commitment need not be disturbed by rationalistic decision procedures. Self-attribution generates a feeling of being in control which makes action meaningful. The element of control makes prediction by way of rationalistic decision procedures less necessary.

From a rationalistic point of view, inconsistent organizational ideologies and conflicts may seem reasonable. People recruited into the organization bring with them different ideologies, and if they keep these then the organization has a better chance of understanding a complex and changing environment. Organizations are normally greatly dependent on their environments, so environment-attribution is often accurate. From an action point of view, however, consistencies and self-attribution are more appropriate.

In this chapter ideological conclusiveness and consistency have been discussed. In the next chapter I will turn to ideological complexity.

Chapter 6

Ideological Change

UP TO NOW OUR DISCUSSION HAS CENTRED ON organizational change actions that are consistent with existing organizational ideologies. These actions can be co-ordinated by conclusive and consistent organizational ideologies. But there are other kinds of change actions — those which are radical enough to be inconsistent with existing ideologies. In this chapter the kinds of ideology that promote such change actions will be examined.

6.1 IDEOLOGICAL COMPLEXITY AND IDEOLOGICAL CHANGE

Conclusive and consistent ideologies facilitate organizational action, but they also seem to narrow the range of such actions. The more conclusive and consistent the ideology, the more exclusive it will be. It might seem dangerous for organizations in changing environments that call for radical adaptive action, to be subject to narrow ideologies of this kind. After all, under inconclusive and inconsistent ideologies a greater number of change actions would be acceptable.

But thinking big is not the same as acting big. Inconclusiveness and inconsistency may promote ideas for change actions but they do not encourage their achievement. On the contrary, radical organizational change actions also require conclusive and consistent organizational ideologies. There appears to be a dilemma here: radical changes seem to make conflicting demands on organizational ideologies. The permissive company and the Runtown case both suggest that inconclusiveness and inconsistency do not solve the problem of achieving radical change.

But the dilemma has a solution. If radical change actions are preceded by ideological shifts, they can then attract enough support to be accomplished. This implies that radical change actions should wait until new ideologies have been established.

121

These new ideologies should still be conclusive and consistent, but the content will have changed.

Ideological Change

The probability of radical change action thus depends on the probability of ideological change. It becomes important to study why, and how, organizational ideologies change. These questions range widely enough to fill several research programmes, but our present discussion will be limited to a study of the aspects of the organizational ideology itself that either favour or discourage its ability to change.

A plausible hypothesis is that the structural characteristics of ideologies that favour organizational action would also favour ideological change. The more conclusive the ideology, the easier it is to see that it is wrong. For example, if reality is described in very precise and unambiguous terms, then many environmental changes will also change the description. Descriptions in very broad and ambiguous terms exhibit a stronger resistance to change, since almost any new situation will be consistent with the existing description. The realization that an ideology is incorrect is an incentive for changing it; the realization that it is correct provides no incentive to change anything.

Furthermore, if organizations have highly consistent ideologies, they can be expected to try to form new consistent ideologies if they perceive changes in reality. Organizations with persistently inconsistent ideologies show great tolerance of inconsistency; changes in reality may simply mean that a different aspect of their ideology appears more accurate and another less accurate than before. Changes in reality may make the ideologies inconsistent in a different way, but they do not mean that an ideology switches from being highly consistent to being highly inconsistent and there will not therefore be any great incentive to change it,

But complexity also becomes crucial. A complex ideology contains many factors and many causal links between its elements, which means that there are several descriptive explanatory statements that can be checked against reality. Changes in reality then provide an incentive to make an ideological shift. The more factors an ideology covers, the more likely it is that some of them will change; and the greater the number of causal links between these factors, the more repercussions there will be from a change in any one of them.

Thus conclusiveness, consistency and complexity together make reactions to changes in the environment more probable. The most stable ideologies are simple ones which are both vague and widely applicable—such as 'our goal is profitability'. A company which regards itself as a transportation company may be no more flexible than one which sees railways only as its domain. The cases presented in Section 5.1 illustrate these effects. The objective ideology of the innovative company had actually changed over time, thus making radical changes possible. All the assumptions about customer behaviour which motivated the product organization, for example, were tested almost daily in contact with customers. Previous assumptions had proved obsolete and had been changed. The permissive company had changed its objective ideology very little since first formulating it. In the case of some of the most important aspects of the ideology, it is even difficult to conceive of any change; what changes in the real world could make it wrong to develop profitable products?

The complexity of its ideology was one reason why the innovative company did not have to be so anxious to select the right projects at the decisive moment, but could transfer part of its choice to later phases. In organizations with complex indeologies, failures may be used as a source of learning. A failure can be interpreted by the ideology, can demonstrate deficiencies in it, and can lead to ideological change. But in organizations with very simple ideologies, failures cannot usually be used in this way. Failures are purely negative and should be avoided at all costs, so that it is very important to choose the right actions and equally natural to use rationalistic decision procedures in doing so.

In Runtown, as in the permissive company, general goals remained unchanged. In other parts of the ideologies, the inconsistencies reinforced the social and ideological situation. In fact, the only major ideological change that could be observed in Runtown concerned an important part of the objective ideology on which all agreed: that it would be possible to attract new companies to the town. Some time later all the parties agreed that, given the situation, this was impossible after all. In this respect the ideology changed from one consistency to another; in all other respects (except goals) it remained inconsistent.

If ideologies are to serve as a basis for choice, they must resist pressure for change and they must change slowly. Indeed, the slow pace of ideological shifts can explain the long time-lags before organizations respond to major threats in their environment, even when the threats seem obvious to external observers (Starbuck et al., 1978).

The need for complex, conclusive ideologies that shift explains the 'myth cycles' reported by Jönsson and Lundin (1977). These authors found that organizations jumped from one dominant ideology or myth to another. Under normal conditions, belief in a dominant ideology is strong, and it will be questioned only during a crisis. When organization members lose faith in a dominant ideology, they replace it by another. The existence of such myth cycles suggests a firm belief in the single objective ideology and in consistency between subjective and objective ideologies, which seems irrational from a decision-making point of view. On the other hand, the cycles allow considerable action rationality: a dominant ideology maximizes the organization's ability to act. Consensus and strong adherence to one ideology are not merely the result of weaknesses in analysis or perception; they are necessary conditions of organizational survival.

Thus the same aspects of the organization that promote organizational actions also promote ideological shifts. Paradoxically, the refining and elaborating of ideologies are steps towards abandoning them. However, the situation in which a change is initiated need not have much in common with the situation in which the change actually occurs. Existing ideologies are threatened when their implications contradict observations. If these threats cannot be met by making the ideologies more ambiguous and broad, inconsistencies will arise between the subjective and objective ideologies and confidence in the objective ideologies will decline. Diverse subjective ideologies may appear, and these may correspond to social structures which differ from those on which the ideologies were founded. There is thus inconsistency between the organization's social and ideology structures, an inconsistency which allows less scope for compromise and authority. As the Swedish Steel case shows, differences between what people think privately and the ideologies to which they can publicly refer are a ready source of misunderstanding. When people misinterpret one another's words, conflicts arise; they escalate and become increasingly difficult to resolve. Once objective ideologies have been questioned, many people see an opportunity to change the organization's environment or its internal functioning, and even their own positions. The gap widens between what 'is' and what 'should be' with regard to goals, methods and the appropriate seat of control. The reader may recognize all these effects from the Runtown case, where the social deadlock was partly due to the abandonment of an objective ideology. Thus ideological shifts and social deadlocks reveal powerful similarities. They both provide a very poor context for action. Ideological inconsistencies increase uncertainty and make it extremely difficult to marshal any commitment to organizational action. Conflict interferes with co-ordination. Consequently, an ideology shift must be completed before the actions begin.

The difference between a deadlock and an ideological shift lies in their stability. A social deadlock is a steady state: it is full of activities, but these activities stabilize the situation, and reinforce the deadlock. A productive ideological shift is a step in a process leading to something new.

This difference between a social deadlock and a productive ideological shift has two implications. The first implication affects the observers of organizational change, who might mistake a confused situation for a productive ideology shift. Since confused situations precede the sort of actions that generate radical change, an observer might infer that confused situations produce change, and that consequently organizations should try to stay confused in order to remain change-prone and readily adaptable to changing environments (Hedberg and Jönsson, 1978). This inference disregards the transitional character of confused situations, and mistakes processes of change of initiators of change. The confused situation during an ideological shift may not resemble either what has gone before or what will come after. On the contrary; conclusive, consistent and complex ideologies provide a good starting-point for ideological shifts as well as a desirable end result. Consensus, rather than conflict, breeds change. Edelman (1971) reports similar results as regards societal ideologies: 'Only mass cognitions that are non-controversial are easily changed' (Edelman, 1971, p. 47).

The second implication is more practical: ideological shifts may become steady states. Social deadlocks are created and maintained by vicious circles in which ideological confusion leads to more confusion, and conflict leads to still more conflict. The confusion and conflict during an ideological shift bring an organization to the brink of social deadlock. How to prevent social deadlocks is an intriguing question for researchers to try to untangle.

6.2 IMPOSED CHANGE — A CASE

A normative conclusion of the hypothesis put forward in the previous section seems to be that organizations striving for change should build up conclusive, consistent and complex ideologies. But this recommendation may seem contradictory to the experience of those who have tried to change organizations with 'strong' ideologies of this kind. In the following pages it will be argued that there is in fact a contradiction: ideological characteristics that favour organizational change in line with environmental change, do not necessarily help anyone who seeks to change an organization in a specific direction desired by himself but not by the organization. Even if an organization may be apt to change, the changes may not necessarily be easily controlled (March, 1981). A distinction should be made between *adaptive change* which stems from the organization's own ideologies and *imposed change* which is generated by, and starts from, different ideologies and is inconsistent with at least the major part of the organization's ideologies.

The case

The following case provides an illustration of imposed change. The organization concerned is the audit department of the administration in one of the largest cities in Sweden. The department had about forty employees and its main activity was to audit the accounting statements of all the units in the administration. The department was organized in two sections, each covering half the city administration. Section AA reported to four groups of politicians, each of which was responsible for its own part of the administration. Section MA reported to three similar groups. By scrutinizing accounting reports and vouchers, the auditors could detect errors which might signal a misunderstanding of the accounting systems, the inefficient use of money, or even illegal behaviour. The department regarded itself as a pioneer; in the late 1960s they were among the first to eliminate the scrutiny of all vouchers by the introduction of sampling methods. In the early 1970s they began to use auditing routines adapted to computerized systems, and at about the same time they launced 'deep audits' which checked the efficiency of a wide range of routines.

By the mid-1970s there was one type of audit that had still not been included in programme — the management audit which had already become an important part of the work of the State Auditing Bureau. Most people were unclear about the purpose and role of management auditing. The State Bureau claimed that the function of management auditors was to check the general effectiveness of public organizations. Researchers in the field argued that trying to audit effectiveness was an impossible task, and that management audits could instead report alternative perspectives on the problems and activities of the organizations concerned. The alternative perspectives would improve the basis for political control over the administrative organizations and provide a stimulus for change in them.

In either case the management audit would call for considerable motivation and commitment on the part of the auditors, in particular at the introductory stage. Like all audits, management audits represent a source of potential conflict with the organizations being audited. Even open conflict could be expected. But unlike accounting audits, management audits could not be supported by clear indisputable norms. The very idea of the management audit was vague and would probably be unfamiliar to most of the people who were to be audited. Under these circumstances, strong and unanimous support among the auditors themselves was extremely important if it was going to be possible to implement the new action. Besides, internal support would be necessary in order to gain the support of the politicians.

Without knowing very much about management audits, the head of the audit department declared that a management auditor position should be established. This was accepted in 1976, and a young university graduate was appointed. The idea of management auditing was actively supported by some of the auditors — as well as by the new employee, of course. These advocates argued that a higher proportion of total resources should be used for management auditing, which was a new and important field.

Now the problems began. What was the newcomer to do? What was a management audit to involve? How should management audits be organized? The first problem to be tackled was this last, and the first solution was to let section MA specialize in management audits, while section AA continued to do accounting audits. The department was divided according to function rather than audited organizations, and as some employees were unwilling to change sections this principle could not be applied throughout. Thus the management audit section continued to do the accounting audit for two groups of organizations. The members of the management audit section consisted of people who actively supported the new idea (the 'advocates') plus a few others.

Section MA did not spend much time planning, but soon started a management audit project in one of the largest of the city's organizations, the Youth Welfare Department. This was one of the organizations for which the section had both the accounting and management audit task. In several other organizations where it was to make only the management audit, projects were planned, and one of them was actually started. Here, the problem of separating the management audit from the accounting audit made it necessary to co-operate with section AA to decide what belonged to which audit. It was also necessary to agree on a concerted approach to the organizations concerned, as they would see no difference between an accounting and a management audit and would not be interested in coping with two teams of auditors at the same time. Co-operation was also desirable, because section AA's familiarity with the 'clients' would be useful in planning and executing the management audits.

But the management audits came up against serious problems. Only the audit of the Youth Welfare Department was ever completed (albeit not very successfully), while the others were either never started or were discontinued. Attempts at co-operation between the two departments failed, since they could never agree about what management auditing really meant, or what action it would involve. The completed project received very little internal support, and its purpose and methods were questioned and criticized.

From this experience two conclusions were drawn. First, almost all organization members thought it was necessary to change the organization chart. A new formal organization was quickly decided and put into effect. As before, both sections were to work for various groups of organizations. The difference was that both sections were now to do both accounting and management audits.

Secondly, the advocates of the management audit idea in section MA realized that they must clarify the meaning of the management audit idea in much greater detail. They also decided that they would have to convince others of the importance of the management audit, so that it would be given high priority and a greater share of resources. They started an intensive and extensive propaganda campaign lasting almost two years. They argued over lunch and during coffee-breaks, and a series of internal conferences was held on the subject.

The propaganda had different effects on different people. The propagandists themselves acquired a much clearer and more complex picture of the management audit. Their enthusiasm for the idea grew. But on most other organization members the propaganda had the opposite effect. Their doubts grew stronger and their criticism more fierce. Many of them argued that management audits were meaningless, and in any case should not be carried out by the audit department. Internal support for management audits diminished rather than increased, which made audit projects difficult even for the keenest advocates of the system. Moreover, they had difficulty in getting external political support for their idea. In section AA no management audits were started. Discussion only made the differences of opinion more obvious, leading to several quite serious conflicts. The internal climate deteriorated. Many of the opponents felt threatened by the new ideas and the advocates felt frustrated by the resistence they encountered.

The introduction of management audits had proved to be an organizational action. Other personnel apart from those initially involved had to participate, to enable the department to introduce management audits as part of its tasks. Active support from the organization was needed, even for the advocates' own projects. The advocates' attempt to isolate themselves and start a project without securing active organizational support, did not become a step towards the full introduction of the new activity. Instead it revealed that a management audit programme did not fit into existing organizational ideologies; it required a different ideology. Thus an ideological shift had to be the first step. But attempts to bring about such a shift also met with major obstacles. The change intended was great — there were big differences between the existing ideology and an ideology that supported management audits.

Differences between ideologies

The existing organizational ideology had a normative focus, being concerned with what the organization should do and how it should do it. Very clear rules were given; acceptable objectives and procedures were precisely indicated. There was almost no inconsistency between description and prescription; the organization was considered to be fulfilling its tasks. Causal linkages were less well developed. Rather, procedures and objectives were based on identification and comparison with similar organizations in other towns, in the state system, and in the private sector. 'We do what they do and we often do it better.' There was not much analysis of the purposes of existing behaviour. Audits were generally geared to discovering errors in order to help people to behave more carefully in the future and to punish and prevent immoral or illegal behaviour. In addition, audits were intended to save the city money. The auditors might come up with less costly procedures for purchasing, contracting, etc.

Clarity was also a feature of the auditing methods used. The 'police' function which the ideology assigned to the auditor made clarity necessary: the auditor had to be able to distinguish clearly between right and wrong. When he criticized an organization he had to have the support of firm unambiguous norms. The establishment and application of such indisputable norms was crucial. The auditors were the experts vis-à-vis the organization they audited, and they were experts in norms.

The idea underlying the management audit was completely contrary to the fundamental idea of the accounting audit. The auditors could not possibly act as management experts in all the diverse organizations they dealt with. No clear predominant norms existed, prescribing what was right or wrong. Instead the audits could provide a basis for discussing possible appropriate norms for the organization being audited. Thus the audit organization needed to accept an ideology in which the auditors were not seen as either experts or policemen, in which they had no fixed norms to support them, in which methods could differ widely, and in which the goal was not to save money but to help the politicians to exert control and to help the organizations to change.

The new ideology differed from the existing one not only in content but also in structural characteristics. The new ideology was very inconclusive, especially compared with the existing ideology: it gave little guidance about how specific management audits should be carried out in practice. The new ideology provided no opportunities for identification: there were few if any similar activities in other municipalities to offer comparisons. Instead it generated motivation by complex references to the need for political control and organizational change. Unlike the existing ideology, it said more about desired states than about the procedures that should be used to attain them.

Strategies for change

In principle there are two ways of promoting an ideological shift: fortifying the new ideology and weakening the existing one. The advocates in the audit department used both methods.

The new ideas were critized for their ambiguity. The attempts to launch management audit projects can be seen as a way of fortifying the new ideology. By demonstrating what the new ideas could mean in practice, their advocates tried to counteract the ambiguity argument. However, the concrete projects simply showed some people that management audits were not what they had expected; they were much more difficult, and made these people appear more inexperienced and incompetent than they had expected to be. Moreover the difficulties that the projects encountered due to opposition, added to the initial resistance.

Another way of reinforcing the new ideology was by referring to the new local government law. This contained one vaguely formulated clause which stated the 'auditing of general management' was to be put into operation. In the existing ideology law was an important part of the environment. The advocates referred to this clause but met with little understanding. They also tried to get support from another part of the department's environment, namely the politicians. This attempt was not very successful either.

Towards the end of the process, the advocates tried a fourth strategy. They started discussing the history of the audit department, trying to discover what changes had occured and why. These analyses could then be used as a platform for discussing the changes now being proposed. The discussion of historical events turned out to be much less tense than the more direct methods that had been tried before. The advocates even got their opponents to take part in writing the history of the department. But by that time the opposition to the management audits had hardened, and the historical discussion did not succeed in softening them up.

The advocates also thought it necessary to take active steps to weaken the old ideology. They described it as old-fashioned and inappropriate, and large parts of the accounting audit as meaningless. Auditors should act as aides, not as policemen. The task was not to distinguish right from wrong but to provide information as a basis for change and political control. The accounting audit was not nearly as advanced or as demanding an assignment as the mangement audit.

Strategies against change

While resistance to the execution of management audits was fairly passive, resistance to the new ideology behind them was stronger and more active. Since the new ideology largely contradicted the existing one, the arguments in its favour were perceived as criticism. The new ideology even made previous behaviour seem meaningless. The accounting auditors felt that if the new ideas were correct, then large parts of their professional life had been useless. This feeling was aggravated by the advocates' attempts at direct criticism of the old ideology and the old behaviour.

Resistance was manifest in four strategies. One was to 'define away' the new ideology. The opponents argued that if managment audits were based on these new ideas, they could not be the task of an auditing department. In other words the old ideology was used to evaluate the new one, and the organization's tasks were defined in terms of its existing ideology. The mere presentation of a new ideology or a new task could not change either the ideological situation or behaviour.

A second resistance strategy was to redefine the new ideology. Instead of claiming that it was too different to be accepted, the new ideology was said to be no different from the existing one. It was claimed that the ideas were not new, but had been there all the time and had resulted in the desired behaviour. Management audits in various versions had existed for at least ten years. (The opponents mentioned some accounting audits that had indicated certain shortcomings in administrative routines.)

The third resistance strategy was acceptance. That is to say, the new ideology was accepted in discussions and debates, but not in practice. People agreed with the advocated but behaved in accordance with the old ideology. By separating the new ideology from their actions, people rendered themselves immune to ideological influence.

The fourth strategy was a variant of the third. People agreed that perhaps the new ideology was right and should be implemented, but unfortunately certain other activities had to have priority. Accounting audits had to be carried out: the law, the demands of the politicians, or some other external and imperative circumstances over which the auditors had no control — all these required it. Management audits could not be justified on the basis of any such pressures.

6.3 ANALYSIS—IDEOLOGY AS LEGITIMATION OF THE PAST

The resistance strategies were effective. They prevented an ideological shift. The old ideology persisted and management audits were not supported, were barely accepted, and were not carried out by anyone except the advocates themselves. The advocates concluded that the only way to achieve change would be to wait for the retirement of their opponents and to successively employ new people whose roots were not in traditional auditing. The opponents concluded that management audits could and should be avoided, and that it was important to stick to traditional routines. The attempts to achieve organizational change had failed.

The advocates tried to introduce a change which was inconsistent with existing ideologies. Existing ideologies were extremely conclusive and consistent, specifying clearly what people should do. And the arguments supporting such actions were clear, logical and agreed upon. The new action required different organizational ideologies. Its advocates faced the problem of changing both ideologies and behaviour. They tried different ways of timing ideological change and behavioural change.

The timing of change actions and ideological shifts

Different ways of timing ideological and behavioural change are illustrated in Figure 6.1. An ideological shift may precede the change action. This is how the adaptive radical changes were brought about in the innovative company described in Chapter 5. Another way is to try to achieve the change action first, without bothering about the need for ideological change or hoping that the change action itself will led to such a change.

This was the technique used at first by the advocates of management auditing. In full accord with the arguments propounded in Chapter 5, this attempt failed. The second technique tried by the advocates was to change ideology and action at the same time (type 3 in Figure 6.1). They tried to change the ideology, but the change was based on a ready-made idea of new action, and one which had already been tried in practice. The new ideology was regarded by everyone as closely connected to the specific change action.

This last technique encountered significant problems. People had to assess a new ideology as well as a very specific action connected with it. If they did not like the action, they intended to reject the ideology. This contrasts sharply with a situation of type 1, in which the exact implications of a new ideology may not be recognized when the ideology changes, particularly if the new ideology is inconclusive. In such a case different people can draw different conclusions. Each participant may believe or at least hope that the new actions arising from the shift in ideology will be favourable, or at least not unfavourable, to themselves. These inconsistencies in perceived implications can persist even after the basic facets of the new ideology have been accepted. By the time the implications prove unfavourable to some people, it may be too late. In the present case a management audit had already been tried and it was easy to assess the effects of this type of action on different people and groups. For example, a few

1 Changing ideology → changed actions
2 Changing actions → changed ideology
3 Changing action + changing ideology → changed ideology and actions.

Figure 6.1   Timing of change of ideology and change of actions. Three techniques

people who expressed a definite wish to participate in management audits at an early stage were denied the opportunity, since they were not considered competent enough. These people could hardly be expected to support the new ideas later.

Communication problems

Some of the problems facing the advocates of management auditing had nothing to do with the timing of ideological change and change actions. They were part of the fundamental problem of communication between two parties upholding different ideologies.

An organizational ideology is the perspective on the basis of which the organization perceives and assesses not only possible actions but also other parts of its world. This world includes new ideas, perspectives and ideologies. Organizations assess new ideologies on a basis of those they already possess. If the opposite were true, and new ideologies were assessed on their own merits then ideological shifts would be less problematic. Instead basic communication problems arise between those who favour a new ideology and those whom they try to convert to it. If the enthusiasts for the new ideology use arguments from the ideology itself and criticize the old ideology from the same standpoint, while the opposing party uses the existing ideology as its reference, it is highly probable that each party will simply become increasingly convinced of its own rightness. The probability of their being able to convince each other is very small (cf. Ross, 1977). The futility of attempts to convince people holding one ideology on the basis of another has been discussed in another context by Feyerabend (1975).

In this perspective advocates of the management audit were

almost bound to fail, given the strategies they used. One strategy was to demonstrate the new ideology and to argue in its favour largely on its own grounds. For example, it was argued that the politicians had a problem of control which should be solved. This strategy was not very effective, however, since the auditors did not consider it relevant to their task to solve the politicians' problems. The strategy did not convince people that a change should be made. The other strategy was to criticize the existing ideology. But from the perspective of the existing ideology, nothing had occurred that could justify a change. It was not reality that had changed; it was being argued that the ideology was wrong.

So the auditors could not be *convinced* of the need to change their ideology. But could they be *persuaded* to change it? What were the chances that they might just accept the new ideology without believing in the arguments? The answer is that the chances were very slight, because of the historical function of ideologies. Ideologies do not only provide a basis for present and future organizational actions. They also provide legitimation of past actions. The conclusiveness and consistency of the existing ideologies of the audit department were not only a good basis for future action, they also legitimized the past. The new ideology would provide no such legitimation. The auditors felt that much of their previous professional life was being retrospectively deprived of meaning.

The counter-strategies also illustrate the communication problem. Either the new ideology was defined as irrelevant to the work of the audit department, or it was interpreted in terms of the existing ideology in a way that implied no change. The 'acceptance' strategies were a way of pretending to be convinced, in order to avoid further attempts at persuasion — a way of remaining ideologically unaffected.

Refining and developing existing ideologies

In order to avoid communication problems, it is possible to promote an ideological change by arguing on a basis of existing ideologies instead of presenting new ones. It is not claimed that existing ideologies are wrong, but that they can be refined and developed. Ambiguous concepts can be clarified or broad ones narrowed down, inconsistencies can be removed and complexity added in the shape of new elements and interrelations.

But the ideologies in the audit department were too conclusive and to consistent to permit much refinement. On the other hand the ideologies were simple; there thus remained the responsibility of adding complexity to them. This was tried by the advocates of the new system by introducing a historical dimension. By examining the origins of the various ideologies and past impulses to ideological change, they tried to add new ingredients and an element of casuality to the ideologies, not at first by questioning the normative elements but by discussing why there were and why there should be rules.

Making the change adaptive

Once the difficulty of changing conclusive, consistent and complex ideologies is accepted, the next step might be to look for ways of stimulating change action within the framework of existing ideologies. This means making the imposed change resemble an adaptive one.

The conclusiveness and complexity of the auditors' ideologies made it difficult for the advocates of change to apply a strategy of refinement, but it meant that the existing ideologies might be fairly adaptable to environmental changes. On the other hand the number of perceivable environmental changes was small, since the ideology was simple. Nevertheless the advocates found one change in a crucial area of the auditors' environment, namely the law. They drew attention to the relevant change in the new legislation. However, this change proved to be too ambiguous to be effective.

6.4 CONCLUSIONS

This case illustrates a failure. Several explanations can be given as to why the advocates of management auditing failed to introduce the change action. The most important explanation was probably that the timing of the attempts to change action and to alter ideologies was wrong. In addition, the attempts at developing the existing ideology came after the new ideology had already fallen into disrepute, and the new legal clause was too ambiguous to elicit a change.

But the case illustrates some possible change strategies, and the kind of difficulties they can encounter. It underlines and illustrates the hypothesis that conclusiveness and consistency do not provide a good basis for imposed change, but that simplicity does. Ambiguity permits new interpretations, breadth permits the stressing of particular aspects, simplicity permits a more complex ideology, and inconsistencies permit the selection of appropriate sub-ideologies when arguing for consistency.

Similar findings are reported by Zajonc (1960) in a study of cognitive tuning in communication. Zajonc found that individuals who expect to be senders of information have more unified, organized and complex cognitive structures than those who expect to be receivers. A good receiver should be open to such information as clarifies his existing cognitive structure and adds complexity to it.

Legitimation and change

By definition the need for imposed changes cannot be derived from existing ideologies. If an imposed change is to be ideologically supported, it therefore requires an ideological shift. The conditions for an imposed ideological shift are different from those of an adaptive ideological shift. Organizational ideologies do not only serve as a basis for future action, they also function as legitimators of past actions. Their legitimation function becomes crucial in the case of imposed changes.

When ideological change arises from a confrontation between existing ideologies and changing environments, past actions do not have to be explained as mistakes. They can be understood and legitimized by reference to the environment as perceived at that time. Changes in environment justify changes in ideology and action. If the new ideology does not evolve from the old one, past actions may easily be perceived as unintelligible or wrong in the light of the new ideology. Even the old ideology itself may be regarded as wrong or mistaken. The need for legitimation makes the imposition of ideological shifts particularly difficult. As in the case of adaptive change, the characteristics of existing ideologies affect the possibility of change.

However, the demands that imposed changes make on organizational ideologies seem to be in complete contrast with the demands made by adaptive changes. Ideologies which are open to adaptive change are not easily altered by an imposed change, and vice versa. This reflects an important distinction between organizations that are 'change-prone', adaptive or changeful and those that are 'change-imposable', manipulable or changeable. The adaptive, changeful organization changes itself in conformity with changes in its environment, but it may seem hopelessly rigid to an external agent who tries to change it in a direction diverging from its own logic. To this agent the other 'changeable' or manipulable kind of organization seems much more apt to accept change. However, the manipulable organization, left to itself, will have much more difficulty in adapting to a changing environment. Something quite different is required of an organization if we want to change it, compared with if we want it to change.

The audit department was an example of an organization which was not very changeable but which had a somewhat better chance of being changeful. If we regard the unions in SSAB (Chapter 4) as a single organization, then this organization could be described as highly changeable. Its lack of any complex ideology connected with the structural problems of the company made it easy to impose management's ideology on it, thus achieving the change action. The inconsistent ideologies among the politicians in Runtown (Chapter 5) made it possible for the local officials to increase their influence and finally to impose some action.

'Changeful' and 'changeable' organizations

Figure 6.2 provides a summary of the discussion above. A 'strong' ideology, i.e. an ideology which is conclusive, consistent and complex, allows variety in the environment to enter and affect the organization. The ideology represents a sensitive picture of reality. Change in the environment stimulates organizational change. On the other hand, the ideology provides a hard shell against external manipulation. A 'weak' ideology, i.e. an ideology which is inconclusive, inconsistent and simple, serves as a buffer between the environment and the organization. The picture of reality is vague and generalized. Signals from the environment do not

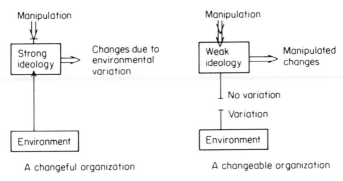

Figure 6.2 'Changeful' and 'changeable' organizations

reach the organization with enough clarity to trigger a response. But the soft shell leaves the organization vulnerable to manipulative attacks.

The source of control is likely to be different in the two types of organization. Changeful organizations can be controlled by their environments, while hierarchic control is more appropriate to the changeable organization. It has been argued that in many organizations new leadership is a prerequisite, or at least a strong stimulus, of change. This might be true for changeable organizations. Putting in a new management seems to be a reasonable step to take in a company which has not proved sufficiently changeful. A new management can easily accomplish change. However, if future changefulness is desired and is actually created, it will have to be accepted that subsequent alterations in management will not lead to change so easily. The different kinds of organizational control are particularly important in political organizations, which will be treated in the next chapter.

Chapter 7

Change actions in Political Organizations

IN PREVIOUS CHAPTERS IT HAS BEEN ARGUED THAT organizational ideologies are major determinants of organizational actions and organizational change. Strong ideologies favour organizational actions and adaptive ideological change, while weak ideologies are more receptive to imposed ideological change.

There is a tendency in organizations to form fairly strong organizational ideologies. Ideological consistency, even in relatively conclusive and complex ideologies, is promoted in several ways. Organization members are induced to think similarly and to recognize their ideological similarities with the help of recruitment policies, interaction with other personnel and common experiences, and as a result of previous efforts to achieve organizational action or to create objective ideologies by the open declaration of policies or strategies. In many organizations there is also a unitarian culture, i.e. the principle of organization is based on the idea of unity: members are supposed to accept certain general goals for the organization and to work for them. Conflict may arise, but should be avoided. Unity is often achieved by way of a hierarchy; some members formulate, propagate and control the basic organizational values.

Unitarian organizations may also contain counteracting forces created by organizational differentiation and departmentalization (Lawrence and Lorsch, 1969). But in some organizations the counteracting forces are part of the organization's basis for legitimating itself. This is true of political organizations, for example a local government led by a council with members from several parties. In such political organizations there is a quest for ideological inconsistency.

In a political organization people are recruited on the grounds that they do *not* share some of the values which are

149

actively supported by other members. Here, disagreement or conflict is the principle of the organization. Conflict is not only a basis for recruitment, it is also something which has to be maintained. Conflict is not dysfunctional; rather, it is a crucial basis for the legitimation of the organization, and there are various techniques for keeping it alive. In other words, this kind of organization institutionalizes conflict.

Political organizations achieve legitimacy by representation, by reflecting different values, beliefs and interests prevailing in their environment. Consequently political organizations ought to develop ideological inconsistency, and preferably even a number of distinct sub-ideologies. These inconsistencies should persist, despite common experiences and interactions among organization members. Moreover, the disagreements should be exposed to external observers. Just as unitarian organizations have various ways of achieving unity and ideological consistency, political organizations can use a number of techniques to make the ideological inconsistencies both evident and persistent.

But many political organizations are set up not only in order to expose conflicts. They are also expected to do and accomplish something, for example to run a town or a company, i.e. their legitimation also stems from the fact that they carry out organizational actions. These 'active political organizations' have two legitimation bases which, as we shall see, make inconsistent demands on them.

Political organizations are probably more common in the public sector, where politicians are supposed to exercise control. Politicians are elected on a basis of observable differences in their opinions. But as a result of a highly selective economic policy and the introduction of industrial democracy, political organizations are becoming increasingly common in the private sector as well. This tendency is very marked in

Sweden, where the strategic actions of many large companies are determined by groups including representatives of top management, the unions, and local and national authorities. The union representatives and the politicians have been included because they are supposed to have ideologies differing from those of top management.

Both the Swedish Steel Corporation (Chapter 4) and Runtown (Chapter 5) are examples of political organizations. These cases also show that a single large organization can contain subunits of the unitarian and political types. In Swedish Steel top management included representatives of management and the unions, while the lower levels were still organized in a traditionally unitarian way. In Runtown there was an administration which was not politically organized. The audit department (Chapter 6) exemplifies a unitarian subunit in a large political organization.

The ideological conditions of the acting political organization make its achievement of organizational change actions particularly difficult, and the techniques which it must use in looking for solutions rather special. Unitarian and political organizations cannot be given the same advice about how to accomplish change. It is thus important to make a separate analysis of the approach to change action in political organizations. This is the theme of the present chapter.

7.1 ORGANIZATIONAL ACTIONS IN POLITICAL ORGANIZATIONS

Active political organizations are under the pressure of two opposing forces. Their organization principal produces a strong dissolving force—the quest for ideological inconsistencies and conflicts tends to dissolve the political organization. If the dissolving force is strong, the organization may no longer be an acting unit to which the label 'organization' is appropriate. Instead it could perhaps be regarded as an arena where other organizations (e.g. parties) or individuals act and counteract. The dissolving force stems from the political element in the organization's legitimation basis — the duty to represent the different values and beliefs of those represented (voters, employees, etc.) But organizational actions benefit from ideological consistency and lack of conflict. The quest for action thus leads to an integrative or organizing force.

The dissolving and integrative forces are inconsistent. If the integrative force is strong, the organization has difficulty in legitimating itself as a political arena; if the dissolving force becomes too strong, it will find it difficult to legitimate itself as an active unit. The active political organization is faced with the problem of being both political and non-political, and of mobilizing for action and being demobilized. It cannot submit to one legitimation basis only; in a political organization where the dissolving force is dominant, the striving for integration becomes important, and in an organization where the integrative force is dominant the striving for dissolution is important.

The quest for politics and the presence of a dissolving force undermine the ability and propensity of the political organization to undertake organizational actions.

A common way of responding to the quest for politics is to let actions be preceded by rationalistic decision procedures. In fact, rationalistic decision procedures are one of the most conspicuous behavioural characteristics of political organizations. Rationalistic decision procedures are sometimes the *result* of disagreement; ideological inconsistencies produce a need for choice prior to the individual action, and rationalistic decision procedures are one way of making choices. They sometimes provide a *method* for disagreement; rationalistic decision procedures are a good way of exposing conflict. They provide an opportunity for indicating possible alternatives to an action, demonstrating advantages and disadvantages and making different ideologies explicit.

Even when the purpose of rationalistic decision procedures is choice, disagreement and uncertainty tend to result. It is difficult to engender strong shared motivation when subjective ideologies are inconsistent. Rationalistic decision procedures seem to be particularly popular when the motivation and commitment of a certain minority are not needed for the action under consideration. Such procedures can then be concluded by voting, which is a further demonstration of disagreement.

Methods of mobilizing organizational action

Rationalistic decision-making represents an obstacle to organizational action. But political organizations can also prepare actions in a more integrative way. When disagreement is bound to arise, political organizations avoid generating motivation first. Bargaining and compromising are examples of this approach. In both cases, one party accepts commitment to an action or part of an action which they do not like, provided that the other party simultaneously commits itself to another action (or part of an action) which the first party favours. The mutual commitment is then supposed to generate enough motivation to launch even those actions (or parts thereof) which are disliked by the actors. However, the amount of motivation achieved can normally be expected to be considerably less than the motivation that can be achieved in an organization with consistent and conclusive ideologies.

Political organizations can also try to overcome their problems with respect to organizational action by structural means. They can separate politics from action, decoupling their attempts to be isomorphic with their environment from their technical core (Meyer and Rowan, 1977). They can respond to the quest for politics by demonstrating ideological inconsistencies in some situations, while using more consistent ideologies as a basis for organizational action in others.

One strategy involves separating politics and action *over time*. In some periods, the organization responds to the quest for politics, and turns to some arena where the conflicts between individuals, parties or suborganizations can be exposed. There is either no objective ideology (such as a formal policy or strategy), or the objective ideology is weak. The inconsistencies in the subjective ideology represent conflicts in several dimensions, not necessarily only in those traditionally demarcating the different parties or subgroups. The organization may be highly representative, exposing a wide range of opinions among the people it represents. Relations to the electorate are then particularly important. Substantial disagreement is made evident. Rationalistic decision processes can be the basis for fierce debates. Bargaining and compromises are avoided; voting is important. But the situation does not generate much capacity for organizational action. If decisions involve organizational action, the action tends not to be accomplished.

In other periods, the organization reponds to the quest for action. Disagreement is suppressed whenever it might interfere with organizational action. A strong and consistent objective ideology is sustained, and is used for reaching agreement. The willingness to compromise and bargain is marked. Creating commitment becomes the main activity. The organization becomes strong on action, but weak on representation.

Runtown employed this strategy. During the 1970s the town passed through several cycles from action orientation to politics, two of which are described in Chapter 5. There, the two inconsistent quests for politics and action were part of the subjective ideology (see pp.105–106). The two quests were also represented by different pairs of roles (majority and oppositional versus the role of being factual). Thus during each period when it was responding to one quest, the organization also 'remembered' the opposite quest and the way it could be handled. The incentive to change from one to the other arose from the fact that following one quest made it obvious that the other was not being duly attended to.

Another strategy for separating politics and action is to differentiate *between issues*. Some issues are used by the organization for exposing conflict. The handling of the other issues is geared more towards action. Typically, issues that do not involve organizational action are treated politically. Local government can give rise to many conflicts and debates on issues such as the size of welfare subsidies or the level of taxes and charges. In companies, management and unions can answer for conflict on the wage-level issue. In these cases there is seldom any problem about effecting what is finally decided: in local government a majority vote is normally sufficient. If issues like these are used to meet political demands, then other issues involving complicated and difficult organizational actions can be handled on a basis of more consistent ideologies and in a spirit of conflict-avoidance. This then makes it possible to carry out the actions. Town planning or the restructuring of a company are issues that tend to be handled in this way.

The organization can also choose between politics and action with respect to the different *kinds of environment* with which it interacts. When negotiating with organizations whose ideologies are normally relatively strong, such as companies, local government bodies in Sweden establish committees.

Their meetings are held in private and the usual political conflicts and debates are not supposed to be in evidence. At the other extreme, when facing the highly unorganized electorate, perhaps before an election, ideological inconsistencies are emphasized. If the electrocate becomes more organized, for example into strong pressure groups, the political organization tends to become integrated.

Finally, the organization can separate politics and action *organizationally*. Some parts of the organization can respond to political demands and others to demand for action. For example, local government can contain a number of sub-organizations of varying degrees of unity. The city council is usually the most disunited sub-organization, where different opinions are supposed to be made evident. Its meetings have a value of their own, and not only (some times not at all) as starting-points for action. They are therefore open to the public. The executive or its special sub-committees can then be more action-oriented. Consequently, their meetings are generally private. Whereas the council consists of members from all parties, the executive and the committees might consist of a ruling majority. Many people normally belong to several sub-organizations. The different functions of these sub-organizations are demonstrated by the fact that people tend to behave differently in them. As we have seen, some people in Runtown even voted differently in the executive and in the council. This may have created some problems, but it represented a perfectly rational response to the different functions of the sub-organizations in question. In the council, where the actors felt that action was important, they agreed to certain decisions. Yet they voted against the same decisions in the council because they felt that the function of the council debate and vote was to expose conflict.

A further organizational differentiation between the two

demands involves the creation of special administrative subunits which are not in any way based on conflict or ideological inconsistencies; these can function as unitarian organizations. The administration is then supposed to execute actions, while the political part of the organization can devote itself to exposing conflict. Each responds to different demands on the organization, and each is constructed in such a way as to facilitate their particular task.

7.2 CHANGE ACTIONS IN POLITICAL ORGANIZATIONS

Political organizations have particular difficulty in undertaking organizational action. What can we say about their capacity for organizational change actions?

In one respect political organizations appear to be organized for change. The ideological inconsistencies, the conflicts, and the demand that these should be exposed, all stimulate thoughts of change. Since organization members have different ideas of what the organization should achieve and how its objectives should be attained, there are likely to be at least some members who want to alter the present situation. Political representatives even feel obliged to propose changes, especially if their role has been defined as one of opposition.

But, as we have seen, these very ideological inconsistencies constitute serious obstacles to realizing any change ideas that involve organizational action. The various strategies that involve separating politics and action increase the ability of the political organization to take organizational action. The separation of politics from actions—over time, between different issues, interaction with different parts of the environment, or organizationally—can facilitate organizational action in some situations. But the separation of politics and action also means that situations in which change action would be easy to achieve are not always the same as the situations in which change actions are easily conceivable. Moreover the political debate often involves proposed change actions, and change actions are good weapons for exposing conflict. So it is not very likely that organizational change actions can be protected from politics, and their chances of being realized are thus reduced.

One way of trying to overcome the difficulties involved in introducing change actions is to form a strong majority. This is fundamentally a variant of the separation of politics and action over time.

The point of a strong majority is that it temporarily determines the struggle for power. It is an attempt to determine whose ideology is to govern a whole range of decisions on one occasion. Compromises, which tend to reduce the degree of change, can be avoided. There is a guarantee that successive actions will be consistent, so that together they may constitute a major change.

The weaknesses of this strategy are as well known as the strategy itself. Strong majorities do not eliminate conflict, criticism, multi-ideological perspectives or decision-making procedures. They can only weaken their impact somewhat. Expectation may be roused on a basis of the majority opinion. Strong commitment may only be needed within the majority. But the problems of uncertainty and motivation remain. Any ideas for change produced by the opposition are systematically disregarded as possible initiators of change actions. The main change initiator is likely to be majority changes. But there are great temptations and sometimes good opportunities for hindering the source of variety in order to avoid majority changes.

The observation that political organizations are often inflexible and unable to instigate major changes is by no means new. The behaviour of these organizations has been described as incrementalistic; revolutions are avoided and the organizations move in small steps (Lindblom, 1959; Braybrooke and Lindblom, 1963). The argument propounded here is that this tendency is due to inherent characteristics in political organizations. Lindblom (1959) claimed that the incrementalistic rational policy in the US made irrational incrementalistic decision-making possible. Since it is possible to change policy only marginally, no comprehensive rational decision-making procedures are necessary. The arguments in this chapter are the opposite of this on two counts. First, decision-making procedures are supposed to influence the ability to change rather than the other way round. Second, it is not irrationality but the relatively high degree of decision rationality in political organization that leads to incrementalism. Political organizations are rational in the sense that they do not believe in a single myth about how the world is, or how it should be. They are rational in the sense that they like to use rationalistic decision procedures before taking specific actions. Unitarian organizations can be much more irrational and are therefore more apt to change.

Other obstacles to change

There are also certain features typical of political organizations, albeit not inherent in them, which influence their ability to change. Normally the members of such organizations are representatives — they are there because they represent a particular interest or opinion. They are supposed to watch over these interests, but they are not usually responsible for what happens to the organization as a whole. In an organization consisting of representatives, there may not be anybody who initiates changes for the organization as a whole.

Many political organizations possess an internal rigidity that obstructs change. Their internal structure has an intrinsic value of its own, and it cannot be subordinated to the need for change. The representatives are not only expected to be in conflict, they are also supposed to represent certain particular conflicts, regardless of whether or not they perceive them as functional and relevant. In a local government organization like the one in Runtown, the politicians are tied to the roles imposed upon them by the most recent election and they cannot abandon the party system even if they all clearly recognize its limitations for solving their problems. The procedures for debate, decision-making and action are fixed. Most organizations in a situation like that of Runtown would have been dissolved. With the help of a new organization it might have been possible to achieve a change. But in many political organizations such a complete reorganization is not permitted, or only with very great difficulty.

The responsibility resting on the representatives may also be unequally shared between success and failure: they may be held more responsible for failure and negative effects than for success and positive effects. Most politicians in the state and local government and most union representatives on company boards, occupy a supervisory role. They are not supposed to run the daily business. This function is delegated to people on a basis of expertise, not of representativeness. The representatives are there to deal with any problems that may arise. As long as everything runs smoothly, they need not interfere. In this situation they tend to be held responsible for such problems as do arise and which they cannot fully solve, while the credit for normal positive developments is given to others.

The institutionalized conflict also reinforces this imbalance in responsibility. Criticism is a major activity. Blame, not praise, is the vehicle of evaluation. There is no one except yourself whose task it is to praise your successes, while there is at least one group whose task it is to blame you for your mistakes. In a political assembly the marketing of the different parties is largely undertaken by their opponents. In most democratic national and local governments, it is the criticism aired by a party's opponents that is observed and efficiently disseminated by the press, not the party's own propaganda.

In such a situation it is not surprising that the representatives become speculators in failure rather than success. It is important to avoid mistakes, but less useful to achieve success. A strategy of caution and passivity develops. Avoiding change is more likely to be rewarding than initiating it.

This biased reward system may lead to a feeling among representatives not only that change is risky for themselves but also that it is not desired by those to whom they are responsible. In a study of politicians in a local government organization (Brunsson and Jönsson, 1979), it was found that all politicians regarded the voters, whom they were supposed to represent, as very conservative. This was probably due to a biased perception of voter attitudes. Each time the politicians initiated or carried through a change, they were met by protests. The change was actively opposed by a minority of perhaps 5 per cent of the population which stood to lose by it. The majority who profited by the change was silent. At the next change another minority protested and so on. The politicians were always meeting strong opposition, but seldom received any very strong support. Even if all changes were accepted by 95 per cent of voters, the politicians might still have been subject to persistent opposition. In such a situation it seems quite reasonable to perceive the voters in general as conservative.

The difficulty surrounding organizational action in political organizations may even lead to a focus on decisions, a state in which the politicians regard decisions rather than actions as their duty. In accordance with the rationalistic ideal, decisions are regarded as destinations and not as starting-points for action. Since decisions are salient in political organizations, it can be tempting to let them become all-important. A decision orientation enables people to make decisions without worrying about any subsequent actions. When actions are independent of decisions, or even non-existent, decision-making becomes much easier. It is even possible to make inconsistent decisions, such as to do and not to do something, and this could be an advantage in an organization with inconsistent ideologies. Decision-makers in this situation need not worry about practical obstacles to action, such as lack of funds, etc.

At one period the politicians in Runtown were clearly decision-oriented. For example, investment projects promised by all politicians during one election campaign were not even included in the subsequent budget. Such behaviour may seem confusing if the politicians are regarded as people strongly geared to action, but from a decision point of view it is obviously rational. Projects proclaimed in the election campaign had already been largely dealt with, i.e. the decision-makers' will to do something had been clearly demonstrated. When the budget was being drawn up a few months later, other projects had come up for decision. Later, projects which had not been considered either in the election campaign or in the budget were given top priority on special lists produced some months after the budget decision. These decisions did not produce any action. It would not have been possible for them to do so: there was enough money for only a few of all the projects decided upon.

A decision orientation may mean that decisions are reached

on many radical organizational changes, but that these are never carried through.

Political organizations and change

To sum up: there are several circumstances which reduce the change capacity of political organizations. Political organizations tend not to be 'changeful', not very ready to adapt to changes in the environment. Changes in the environment tend to be perceived and interpreted differently by members whose ideologies are different, and they tend to give rise to different conclusions. Organizational action is difficult to achieve. Political organizations would have difficulty in surviving in systems where the input of resources depended on the organization's adaptability in terms of change actions. And, sure enough, most political organizations normally receive their resources from budgets or taxes, whereby the resource input can be more easily controlled or directed by the organization itself, and by the organization's legitimacy as a representative political unit and not by specific actions. The Swedish Steel Corporation (Chapter 4) was a political organization that was partly dependent on resources from a market. It was able to adapt to environmental threats, but only by moderating its political character (i.e. by depriving the unions of influence). Even then, adaptation to market conditions was not complete; substantial additional resources were obtained from the national budget.

The only important environmental source of change in a political organization is the election of new representatives, provided the voters are sufficiently independent of the representatives. The most changeful political organizations seem to be those that follow the principle of parliamentarianism, in which the voters often initiate majority shifts.

Sometimes, however, it is not enough for the politicians to initiate a change: the achievement of the change often depends on the efforts of administrative subunits whose members are not recruited on political grounds but who are supposed to be controlled by the politicians. The role of these units will be analysed in the following section.

7.3 ADMINISTRATIVE SUBUNITS IN POLITICAL ORGANIZATIONS

Politics and administration as ideal types

It is common for political organizations to be divided into two parts, one political and one administrative. The political subunit is politically organized and is supposed to control the administrative unit. The administration is organized on unitarian lines and recruitment is according to expertise rather than political representativeness.

This division into political and administrative subunits can be seen as a way of handling the problem of action in political organizations. It means that thinking and acting are organizationally separated. The political unit concentrates on debate and decision-making, while action is delegated to the administration whose internal organization is better suited to organizational action.

However, the picture is rather more complicated than this. Typically the political subunit is supposed to control the administrative subunit. Hence, the political character of the organization as a whole should be guaranteed; the administration is supposed to be an instrument of the political subunit with no independent will or influence of its own. The decisions of the political subunit are supposed to trigger the administrative actions, while any preceding decision-making processes are supposed to be irrelevant to the administration. The decision should produce the expectations, the motivation and the commitment necessary to the implementation of the decision in the shape of an action in the administration.

Ideology can provide a complementary method of control over the administration. If there is a strong political majority which possesses a consistent ideology, control over administrative actions can be acquired by transferring the ideology of the majority to the administration. Expectations, motivation and commitment, too, can then be ideologically based. Both control by decision and control by ideology-transfer make very specific demands on the administrative subunits.

Using the terminology introduced in Chapter 6, the role of the administrative units requires them to be 'changeable' rather than 'changeful'. They should be controlled by the decisions or the ideology of the political subunit, not by material changes in the environment. A new political majority should acquire the same degree of control as the old one.

In order to be changeable, administrations should have weak ideologies. The existence of inconclusive, inconsistent and simple ideologies will make it more probable that political decisions will fit the ideologies or at least will not be contrary to them. Weak ideologies also facilitate ideological manipulation. And since the actions of the administration should be guided not by their own ideologies but by the political decisions, they do not need strong ideologies as a basis for action.

Politics and administration in practice

However, if we leave the ideal state and turn to practice, there seems to be very little incentive for the administrative subunits to develop into changeable organizations, apart from the formal requirement. On the contrary, there are several incentives for developing strong organizational ideologies. First, there are the usual forces in a unitarian organization that generate strong ideologies. Action is facilitated by strong ideologies. At least at the top of the administrative subunits, there may be considerable interest in gaining control over the administrative operation and in overcoming the uncertainty that external control can engender. Ideologies are often reinforced by the recruitment process. Administrative subunits are manned by experts in specific fields. As a result of their training, experts tend to have conclusive, consistent and complex ideologies in connection with their professional area.

The likelihood that the administrative units will be changeable is slight. It is much more likely that the political subunits will be changeable, since the very nature of the political subunits tends to give them weak ideologies. This means that strong forces tend to reverse the direction of contol compared with what is prescribed in the ideal model. It is easier for the administrative subunits to control the politicians than the other way round.

It is not only the general ideological situation of the two subunits that put the administrative units in a stronger position. In practice there may well be other circumstances that add to their powers of control. For example, the political unit is generally dependent on the expertise of the administration when it formulates its decisions. The administration provides action alternatives, ways of describing the alternatives, information about them, and arguments for and against them. The political unit is ready to make its decisions once it has learnt enough to be able to argue in support of them (Brunsson and Jönsson, 1979).

Strong ideologies in the administrative subunit, will

stimulate change actions. But the roles of the political and administrative units complicate things. If the influence of the political unit is slight, it will seldom be able to initiate changes. Even if the political unit perceives the need for change, or changes its ideologies, or achieves majority shifts, there is a good chance that this will not result in new organizational actions. The political unit is far from being the change-initiator prescribed by the ideal model.

Administrative units are not very changeable but their strong ideologies tend to make them changeful. Changes initiated by the administration have a better chance of being completed. And yet the whole question of change is complicated in that the administrators have to convince the politicians in order to elicit their commitment. This may slow down the process of change substantially, and sometimes the commitment may never be obtained.

But these delays also contain activities that can sometimes greatly facilitate radical change. Political organizations dominated by administrative subunits may sometimes prove to be powerful change forces. The commitment on the part of the politicians expressed in their decision is often extremely valuable when carrying through change actions which the environment barely supports or even obstructs. The political decisions legitimate the actions, since they are supposed to express the will of the people whom the politicians represent. Politicians are prepared to accept responsibility for actions by deciding on them when they are able to act as 'senders of information' (Zajonc, 1960) towards those they represent. The politicians can then successfully argue in favour of their decisions. In such cases their role is to defend the actions of the administration and to act as the target for external criticism. The political unit becomes a buffer between the administration and the environment.

Political organizations of this kind may be very changeful. But their behaviour may easily be dysfunctional from a democratic point of view: it is very likely that the changes do not correspond to the wishes of the electorate, but instead are serving the ends of the administration itself. The administration may dominate instead of adapting. Many political organizations work in areas where they have a high degree of autonomy or when they enjoy a monopoly. The political form of organization is often chosen precisely in order to guarantee the influence of the voters on the organizational actions. But instead it may function as a way of guaranteeing influence over the voters. The political unit may still demonstrate conflict, but the conflicts may be questioned if majority shifts fail to lead to different actions, i.e. if a new majority takes over responsibility for the same administrative actions that previous majorities have defended. In the long run much of the political legitimation of the organization may be lost.

The existence of the political unit makes it much easier for an administration to dominate. The two types of organization shown in Figure 6.2, can now be joined by a third type, described in Figure 7.1.

The case of Swedish Steel (Chapter 4) demonstrated the strength of a political organization with a dominant administration in its relations with its environment. At least in Swedish politics, at both the national and the local levels, there are numerous examples of radical changes brought about by the administrative subunits of political organizations, with very little external support. These processes are very difficult to stop or to change, even in the long term. The very long planning periods in turbulent environments—in urban development or investment in energy production, for instance—would probably not be possible for any except

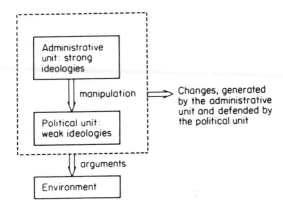

Figure 7.1   A political organization dominating its environment

political organizations dominated by their administrations. In such cases the projects often far outlive the opinions and environmental conditions from which they once sprang. Politicians find themselves defending, and thus permitting, action for which there is now very little general support. Such action would be very difficult for private companies to indulge in, without political legitimation.

So the method of overcoming action difficulties by delegating action to administrative subunits may produce effects contrary to the very idea of the political organization. An important task for researchers and practitioners is to try to find ways of organizing and managing political organizations which preserve their political legitimation and their democratic function and give them a high ability to undertake adaptive change.

Chapter 8

Summary and Implications

THE INVESTIGATIONS REPORTED IN THS BOOK STEMMED originally from an interest in organizational change. But, in order to understand change, it proved necessary to examine and seek to understand the conditions of organizational action. A theory of organizational action based on case studies of organizational change actions has been elaborated in the previous chapters. In this chapter the theory will be summarized and some of its implications for organizational change will be discussed. The first part of the chapter will suggest some answers which the theory can provide, while the second will look at some of the questions that it raises.

8.1 A THEORY OF ORGANIZATIONAL ACTION

Organizational action is action undertaken by several organization members in co-operation with one another. Organizational action is particularly complicated when many people belonging to different parts of the organization are involved. Organizational action can be understood on a basis of three interrelated concepts: motivation, expectation and commitment.

Actors should believe the considered action to be a 'good' one; they should expect it to be carried out by the organization; and they should commit themselves to it. The stronger the motivation, the expectation and the commitment, the more likely it is that people will participate in the organizational action.

But it is not enough for people to be highly motivated, confident in their expectations, and committed; they should be all of these things in relation to the same organizational action. So the problem is to get support for a specific action, support that is sufficiently strong and sufficiently widespread.

173

Part of the solution lies in the interrelations between motivation, expectations and commitment, as these factors tend to influence each other at both the individual and the organizational levels.

Interrelations between motivation, expectations and commitment

On the individual level, motivation tends to influence commitment. People who believe an action to be worthwhile will be more willing to commit themselves to it. They may work actively to get it to happen, thus accepting responsibility for it. Open expression of a positive opinion in itself implies commitment. But commitment also affects motivation: once people have committed themselves to an action, they are more anxious to see it carried out successfully.

Expectation influences motivation. If people do not expect the action to be carried out, it will not seem worthwhile making a contribution. In Chapter 4 it was shown that this factor could also be stated in positive terms: firm expectations could make some people see the action as a good one. Motivation can influence expectations: this relationship can be described as wishful thinking, or as an expression of a tendency to expect other people to react in the same way as oneself (due to consistency between subjective and perceived ideologies).

Expectation influences commitment. It is pointless and possibly even harmful to commit oneself to an action which it is thought may never materialize. If it does not, then blame may attach to the people committed to it. They may be accused of not having tried hard enough.

Other relations operate at the organizational level. Commitment influences expectations. If many important parties commit themselves to an action, people will expect it to be carried out. Commitment on the part of others may also influence motivation either directly or by way of expectations; it makes it worthwhile to make one's own contribution.

Starting-points for actions

To sum up: there is a set of positive correlations between the conditions of action, which can be pictured as in Figure 8.1. The existence of these correlations makes organizational action both simpler and more likely. This does not mean that any one condition can be used to wholly determine the others. But the existence of these interrelations offers organizations an opportunity to start working on one condition and then to influence the others from this starting-point. The cases described in the previous chapter illustrate different starting-points. Rationalistic decision procedures of the kind described in Chapter 3 imply a starting-point in motivation. The idea is to discover and agree on which action is the best (or whether a considered action is good enough). Commitment and expectations can then be formed on a basis of the common motivation for the same action. The case of Swedish Steel in Chapter 4 exemplifies a process that started with the rousing of expectations, which were then used to try to create commitment and, up to a point, motivation. The impressionistic decision mode described in Chapter 3 is a way of starting from commitment, thus producing or reinforcing motivation and expectations.

The cases described gave the following results. Starting from motivation by using rationalistic decision processes produced little in the way of commitment and expectations. Starting with the formulation of expectations, it was difficult, although not impossible, to create commitment and motivation. Starting from commitment proved to be the most effective way of

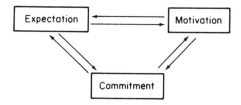

Figure 8.1   Conditions of organizational action and their interrelations

generating the determinants of action, mainly because commitment had a powerful impact on both expectations and motivation. The impact of expectations and motivation on commitment was much weaker.

Uncertainties and conflicts

A further reason why rationalistic decisions do not provide a good basis for action is that although they put great emphasis on the motivation requirement, they tend to produce very little motivation. Instead, they tend to produce uncertainty.

Uncertainty reduces both motivation and expectations. Consequently tendencies to perceive uncertainty are crucial to the organization's ability to take organizational action. Uncertainty is one factor in the risk 'product' (the other is stakes), and risk, too, reduces motivation. The stakes factor in the risk product is dependent on responsibility. So important methods of risk reduction include reducing uncertainty and reducing responsibility. But since the reduction of responsibility also reduces the other conditions of action, a strategy of uncertainty reduction provides a much better basis for action.

Commitment is reduced by conflict. Conflicts are strong and overt dispositions not to help adversaries or even to work against them. Persistent conflict can result in people refusing to commit themselves to common actions. When conflict is severe, there is little point in trying to start from commitment as a platform for organizational action: the conflict is likely to make people evade commitment rather than accept it.

Conflict may be realistic, i.e. based on inconsistencies in people's perceptions and appraisals of situations, in other words on inconsistent subjective ideologies. Or conflict may be unrealistic, expressing frustration and tension. If it is thought that a conflict is unrealistic, it might be tempting to start by working on motivation (as in Runtown), hoping that rationalistic procedures will lead to agreement. If the conflict is realistic (as in Swedish Steel), it might be wise to start by working on expectations. As the cases demonstrate, these tactics by no means guarantee success in rousing strong commitment. Creating compromises is another way of starting from commitment, despite conflict. This tactic is probably most successful in situations of realistic conflict.

Ideologies

Creating commitment is different from creating motivation and expectations in one important respect. Common expectations and common motivations can arise in individual actors without there having been any social processes between them. But commitment is a social activity.

Commitment to certain actions can be created by social processes long before any individual action takes place. By formulating and gaining acceptance for standard operating procedures, organizations can create commitment which functions as the initiator of specific organizational actions in specific anticipated situations. In the case of situations or actions which are not anticipated, this method is not feasible and commitment cannot be created in advance. But expectations and motivation can.

Establishing common expectations and motivation is the function of organizational ideologies. Organizational ideologies increase the likelihood that organization members will expect the same actions and will feel motivated to participate in them.

Organizational ideologies consist of peoples' values and beliefs about the organization and its situation. Organizational ideologies include subjective ideology, that is the sum of peoples' cognitive structures, perceived ideology, that is peoples' perceptions of each others' cognitive structures, and objective ideology, that is the values and beliefs that can be referred to and used as arguments among individuals. Consistency and conclusiveness are important aspects of organizational ideologies. These characteristics determine how much the ideologies will reduce variety. Consistency provides a basis for common motivations and expectations. A highly consistent subjective ideology makes it very probable that people will agree on whether an action is 'good' or 'bad'. If there is a high degree of consistency between subjective and perceived ideologies, people will expect others to be motivated for the same actions as themselves. If the objective ideology is highly consistent with the subjective and perceived ideologies, it will be easy to use it in favour of a preferred action.

If ideologies are very general and vague, it may be easy to achieve the types of consistency described above. However, such ideologies will not provide a good basis for agreement on a specific action. For this, they must also be highly conclusive. Conclusiveness is also important in that it increases the likelihood of strong motivation and firmly held expectations — it reduces uncertainty. Conclusiveness arises from clarity and narrowness (as opposed to ambiguity and breadth). A conclusive ideology tends to give a clear result when it is used to evaluate a proposal for an action, and it tends to lead to the same action ideas in similar situations.

Ideologies should also possess a high degree of perseverance if they are to serve as effective guides for motivation and expectations. Ideologies should survive the action proposal or the situation which produces the action idea. If the proposal or the situation leads people to question the ideologies, then these cannot be expected to serve as the instrument of strong common motivations and expectations. Complexity can increase perseverance. It is probably easier to question simple normative statements about what actions are acceptable, than to question an ideology consisting of many interrelated arguments about why certain actions are acceptable.

Consistent, conclusive and complex ideologies can thus result in strong common motivations and expectations with respect to action proposals, without any special efforts having to be made. 'Thinking' is separated from both commitment-building and action. Action can then start at the commitment end, and the preparation for action can be devoted to the creation of commitment. This tends to be fairly easy, since motivation and expectations are already there. Commitment will then further reinforce them.

Inconclusive, inconsistent and simple ideologies do not provide a good basis for the generation of strong common motivations and expectations. Such ideologies make it difficult to start preparing for action at the commitment end. It might then seem reasonable to start by creating motivation instead. But such a procedure tends to evoke a lot of uncertainty and little commitment, in the specific case where ideologies are weak; the temptation to use rationalistic decision procedures is strong when ideologies are weak.

In addition, inconsistent ideologies easily lead to conflict, and not just in the case of inconsistencies within subjective ideologies. Unrealistic conflicts were created in both Runtown and Swedish Steel as a result of other inconsistencies. In Runtown they arose when people misinterpreted each others' behaviour, because of inconsistencies between subjective and perceived ideologies. In Swedish Steel conflict was generated by inconsistencies between subjective, perceived and objective ideologies.

Change actions

Actions that would involve radical changes in organizational behaviour are generally difficult to carry out and they call for strong commitment, firm expectations, and high motivation; conclusive, consistent and complex ideologies should endorse these actions. But such ideologies constrain the possibility of change, because only changes that match the ideologies receive ideological support.

Changes in conclusive ideologies do sometimes suffice. Often, however, organizations need immediate radical changes in response to rapid environmental change, and conclusive ideologies would rule out any change radical enough to answer such a situation. And yet broad and ambiguous ideologies would not afford a strong basis for action. This is the ideological dilemma: radical changes call for conflicting qualities in the organizational ideologies. There is a solution, however. Again, the trick is to separate thinking from acting. If change actions are preceded by ideological shifts, they can attract enough support to promote their accomplishment. This means that change actions should wait until new ideologies have been established.

If radical changes have to wait upon ideological shifts, it

becomes very important to know how ideologies change. What properties of an ideology make it apt to shift when required? In order to discuss this, it is necessary to distinguish between adaptive changes and imposed changes.

Changefulness and changeability

Adaptive changes arise from the interaction between organizational ideologies and organizational environments. Organizations discover that their environments are changing, and they change their ideologies accordingly. Ideologies that are conclusive, consistent and complex are liable to evolve by way of adaptive change. The more conclusive the ideologies, the easier it is to see that they are wrong. Broad ambiguous ideologies will correctly describe more environmental situations. Low tolerance of organizational inconsistency will make it more difficult to adapt to environmental change by introducing inconsistencies. Complex ideologies make it more probable that environmental changes will be observed, and that they will have strong ideological effects. The conclusion is that ideologies which provide a good basis for organizational action are also prone to change when the environment changes.

Imposed changes stem from sources other than the organization's own ideologies. There is an external or internal agent who wants a change to take place. Inconclusive, inconsistent and simple ideologies will favour imposed change, since they can be specified appropriately by the change agent. Inconsistencies make it possible to choose among several ideological elements from which a consistent ideology can be formed. Simple ideologies can be made more complex by supplying the organization with additional information.

Strong ideologies make organizations more changeful, weak ideologies make them more changeable.

8.2 IMPLICATIONS

Many contributions to management research have ended in a call for more decision rationality and greater broad-mindedness in organizations. The main practical implication of the present study is that some of these arguments should be questioned. My main argument, addressed to practitioners in the field, is that in many situations decision irrationality and ideological narrow-mindedness may be functionally effective. Or, to put it another way, the ideological irrationalities and narrow-mindedness so often observed are not necessarily, or at least not always, effects of organizational stupidity which should be eradicated. Instead rationalism and ideological broad-mindedness should often be avoided.

But organizations sometimes risk reducing their action capacity, even without some outside observer advocating rationality. Organizations which experience failures may, like individuals, increase their environment-attribution (Weiner and Kukla, 1970), or, like groups, they may try to minimize the risk of failures rather than maximize the chance of success (Zander, 1971) or, again like individuals, they may acquire ideologies which are less complex (Streufert, 1973). If they do any of these things, they reduce their ability to undertake the change actions that might be necessary to avoid further failure. A vicious circle may arise, which must be prevented if organizations are to remain viable.

The results reported here also call in question solutions to organizational problems based on the decision paradigm; for example, decision participation may not necessarily be a good way of acquiring influence over organizational actions. The action theory points instead to organizational ideologies as an important target for management control.

According to several authors, top management is able to influence organizational ideologies by a variety of techniques such as planning, strategy formulation, or the design of information systems (Ansoff *et al.*, 1976; Lorange and Vancil, 1977; Starbuck *et al.*, 1978). But the ideologies which are easiest to change from the top are the weak ones, i.e. those which provide a bad basis for organizational action. In some cases it may not be too difficult to inject more strength into a weak ideology, thus providing an ideological basis for action and exercising an influence on the choice of actions to be taken. But once this has been done, the organization will be less open to ideological manipulation since strong ideologies have already been developed. So there seems to be a limit to the ideological control of organizational change actions. It may perhaps be necessary to sacrifice some control ambitions, if the aim is an organization able to undertake organizational change actions. Organizations are not necessarily boundlessly manageable.

Research results also breed new research questions. An obvious question arising from any social science research is how, and how far, the results apply to situations other than those studied. In the present study, a broad range of situations and organizations has been analysed, but further research is needed to develop the theory and refine the concepts further. In particular it would be interesting to give more elaborate answers to questions concerning the interactions between decision conditions and those between uncertainties, risks and stakes. Other interesting questions are: 'How are organizational ideologies created and changed?' 'How important is the historical legitimation function of ideologies, and how does this function interact with their function as a basis for current and future action?' The importance of action rationality and strong ideologies could also be illustrated by comparing the organizational processes studied here with rationalities and ideologies in organizations such as universities, where organizational action has little or no importance as a legitimating instrument.

The further development of concepts could also benefit from comparison with previous research. An interesting parallel with some of the observations presented here can be found in psychological research concerning irrationalities at the individual level, in which the individual's decision-making behaviour is studied in laboratory contexts. The decision-making process described in Chapter 3 is consistent with the findings reported in Slovic (1972), whereby individuals make assessments by anchoring, i.e. they start with a few cues and then add cues in support of the original ones. People have been found to use a few cues only in their assessments; their models of the world were much simpler than they could have been, given all the information that they possessed (Tversky and Kahneman, 1974). In addition, people tend to be overconfident as to their models; they believe their models of the world to be more reliable than they actually are (Fishoff, 1975; Ross, 1977; Lord *et al.*, 1979). Depressed people have been found to be more realistic than others, but also to have difficulty in taking action (Seligman, 1975).

Laboratory experiments on assessments and decision-making are generally performed in such a way as to preclude action, which means that any guess about the extent to which people will apply the same type of reasoning in action situations will be very risky. None the less, with regard to the irrationalities described here, it is tempting to assume that individuals repeat their ways of thinking in laboratories even in real action situations. The irrationalities at the individual level may have the same function that we have assigned to them at the organizational level, namely to smooth the way for difficult actions. Rational thinking may be an obstacle to action on the individual level too. Entrepreneurs are regularly over-optimistic and self-attributing. A new company's chances of success are very slight in many industries, and rational analysis would often yield very low expected values (cf. the rationalistic company's fear of flops in product development, as reported in Chapter 3). Rational thinkers would never start companies in such conditions, but entrepreneurs do.

But the studies presented here are not only the basis for their own further refinement. They also give rise to several questions that would reward further research. The most interesting are probably those connected with the contrast between action rationality and decision rationality.

Action rationality creates expectations, motivation and commitment, all of which make it easy to launch and carry through organizational actions, but it does not provide any incentive for discontinuing them, for instance when environmental changes occur in the course of an action which deprive it of its advantages. Instead organizational actions originally springing from strong expectations, clear motivation and firm commitment may be almost impossible to stop. Decision rationality is a better instrument for halting an organizational action that is already under way. A study of failures and successes in stopping organizational actions is needed to improve our understanding of this problem.

Other important questions concern ideological change. According to the theory presented here, strong ideologies engender action rationality, while ideological changes are important to organizational choice. Can ideological changes be determined by processes imbued with decision rationality? Or are there powerful obstacles to this, e.g. that both old and new ideologies are needed to justify the past and make it meaningful? Can such obstacles be overcome by introducing a new leadership to trigger ideological change? And how do organizations avoid getting stuck in the transition phase between two ideologies, how do they finally develop strong new ideologies instead of becoming trapped in social deadlocks?

Since action rationality is often functionally effective, it is not surprising to find that organizations frequently employ this kind of rationality. It is more surprising to find that even when initiating organizational actions they sometimes appear, at least superficially, to be applying decision rationality. It is not the question of decision irrationality that calls most urgently for investigation; it is decision rationality. What is the function or social meaning of decision rationality, for instance in investment calculations or rationalistic investigation procedures? What are the rationales of rationality in different kinds of organizations?

Political organizations are organizations in which decision rationality may function both as a basis for choice and as a way of exposing conflicts. But in order to accomplish organizational actions, action rationality is required. Political organizations find themselves balancing between the two rationalities. They expose fundamental problems connected with rationality and action and can teach us a great deal about fundamental problems and solutions in organizations. Moreover, political organizations are becoming very common phenomena, often of great practical significance. They deserve much more attention than organization theorists have given them hitherto.

References

Ackerman, B. A., Ross-Ackerman, S., Sawyer, J. W., and Henderson, D. W. (1974) *The Uncertain Research for Environmental Quality*. New York: Free Press.

Aharoni, Y. (1966) *The Foreign Investment Decision Process*. Boston: Harvard University Press.

Ansoff, H. I., Declerck, R. P., and Hayes, R. L. (eds) (1976) *From Strategic Planning to Strategic Management*. New York: Wiley.

Argyris, C. (1977) Organizational learning and management information systems. *Accounting, Organizations and Society*, **2**, 113–23.

Ashby, R. (1956) *Design for a Brain*. London: Science Paperbacks.

Bem, D., Wallach, M., and Kogan N. (1965) Group decision making under risk of aversive consequences. *Journal of Personality and Social Psychology*, **1**, 453–460.

Boulding, K. (1966) The economics of knowledge and the knowledge of economics. *American Economic Review. Papers and Proceedings*, Vol. 56, No 2, 1–13.

Braybrooke, D. and Lindblom, C. E. (1963) *A Strategy of Decision*. New York: Free Press.

Brunsson, N. (1976) *Propensity to Change*. Göteborg: BAS.

Brunsson, N. (1982) Företagsekonomi—avbildning eller språkbildning. In Brunsson, N. (ed): *Företagsekonomi—sanning eller moral*. Lund: Studentlitteratur.

Brunsson, N. and Jönsson, S. (1979) *Beslut och handling*. Stockholm: Liber.

Churchman, C. W. (1964) Managerial acceptance of scientific recommendations. *California Management Review*, **7**, 31–38.

Clark, B. R. (1972) The organizational saga in higher education. *Administrative Science Quarterly*, **17**, 178-84.

Coser, L. (1956) *The Functions of Social Conflict*. Glencoe, Ill: Free Press.

Cyert, R. M. and March, J. G. (1963) *A Behavioral Theory of the Firm*. Englewood Cliffs, N. J.: Prentice-Hall.

Dale, A. and Spencer, L. (1977) Sentiments, Norms, Ideologies and Myths: Their Relation to the Resolution of Issues in a State Theatre Company. Working paper. European Instutute of Advanced Studies in Management.

Danielsson, A. and Malmberg, A. (1979) *Beslut fattas*. Stockholm: SAF.

Downey, H. K., Hellriegel, D., and Slocum, J. W. (1975) Environmental uncertainty: the construct and its application. *Administrative Science Quarterly*, **20**, 613–629.

Downey, K. H. and Slocum, J. W. (1975) Uncertainty: measures, research and sources of variation. *Academy of Management Journal*, **18** (3), 562–578.

Duncan, R. (1972) Characteristics of organizational environments and perceived environmental uncertainty. *Administrative Science Quarterly*, **17**, 313–322.

Edelman, M. (1971) *Politics as Symbolic Action*. New York: Academic Press.

Feyerabend, P. (1975) *Against Method*. London: NLB.

Fishoff, B. (1975) Hindsight and foresight: the effect of outcome knowledge on judgement under uncertainty. *Journal of Experimental Psychology: Human Perception and Performance*, **1**, 288–299.

Galbraith, J. (1973) *Designing Complex Organizations*. Reading, Mass.: Addison-Wesley.

Glaser, B. and Strauss, B. (1968) *The Discovery of Grounded Theory*. London: Weidenfeld and Nicolson.

Goldberg, L. R. (1968) Simple models or simple processes? Some research on clinical judgements. *American Psychologist*, **23**, 483–496.

Hägg, I. and Hedlund, G. (1978) Case Studies in Social Science Research. Working paper. European Institute for Advanced Studies in Management.

Harvey, A. (1970) Factors making for implementation success and failure. *Management Science*, Series B, **16**, 312–320.

Hedberg, B. L. T. and Jönsson, S. A. (1978) Designing semi-confusing information systems for organizations in changing environments. *Accounting, Organizations and Society*, **3**, 47–64.

Hoffman, P. J. (1968) Cue-Consistency and configurality in human judgement. In Kleinmetz, B. (ed.), *Formal Representation of Human Judgement*. New York: Wiley.

Huysmans, J. H. (1970) The effectiveness of the cognitive style constraint in implementing operations research proposals. *Management Science*, **17**, 99–103.

Janis, I. L. (1972) *Victims of Group Think*. Boston, Mass.: Houghton Mifflin.

Jönsson, S. A. and Lundin, R. A. (1977) Myths and wishful thinking as management tools. In Nystrom, P. C. and Starbuck, W. H. (eds), *Prescriptive Models of Organizations*. Amsterdam: North-Holland, 157–170.

Kahneman, D. and Tversky, A. (1973) On the psychology of prediction. *Psychological Review*, **80**, 237–251.

Keeney, R. L. and Raiffa, H. (1976) *Decisions with Multiple Objectives*. New York: Wiley.

Lawrence, P. and Lorsch, J. (1969) *Organization and Environment*, Homewood, Ill.: Richard Irwin.

Leifer, R. and Huber, G. (1977) Relations among perceived environmental uncertainty, organizational structure and boundary-spanning behaviour. *Administrative Science Quarterly*, **22** (2), 587–608.

Lindblom, C. E. (1959) The science of 'muddling through'. *Public Administration Review*, **19**, 79–88.

Lorange, P. and Vancil, R. F. (1977) *Strategic Planning Systems*. Englewood Cliffs, N. J.: Prentice-Hall.

Lord, C., Ross, L., and Lepper, M. (1979) Biased assimilation and attitude polarization: The effects of prior theories on subsequently considered evidence. *Journal of Personality and Social Psychology*.

Lundberg, E. (1961) *Produktivitet och räntabilitet*. Stockholm SNS.

March, J. G. (1978) Bounded rationality, ambiguity, and the engineering of choice. *Bell Journal of Economics*, **9** (2), 587–608.

March, J. G. (1981) Footnotes to organizational change. *Administration Science Quarterly*, **26**, 563–577.

March, J. G. and Olsen, J. P. (eds) (1976) *Ambiguity and Choice in Organizations*. Bergen: Universitetsforlaget.

March, J. G. and Simon, H. A. (1958) *Organizations*. New York: Wiley.

McKelvey, G. and Aldrich, H. (1983) Population, natural selection and applied organizational science, *Administration Science Quarterly*, **28**, 101–128.

Meyer, J. W. and Rowan, B. (1977) Institutionalized organizations: formed structure as myth and ceremony. *American Journal of Sociology*, **83** (2), 340–363.

Mintzberg, H: (1973) *The Nature of Managerial Work*. Englewood Cliffs, N. H.: Prentice-Hall.

Murdick, R. G. and Ross, J. E. (1975) *Information Systems for Modern Management*. Englewood Cliffs, N. J.: Prentice-Hall.

Nebeker, D. (1975) Situational favorability and perceived environmental uncertainty: an integrative approach. *Administrative Science Quarterly*, **20**, 281–294.

Nisbett, R. and Ross, L. (1980) *Human Inference*. Englewood Cliffs, N. J.: Prentice-Hall.

Nyström, H. (1974) Uncertainty, information and organizational decision making. A cognitive approach. *Swedish Journal of Economics*, 131-139.

Prest, A. R. and Turvey, R. (1965) Cost-benefit analysis: a survey. *Economic Journal*, **75**, 685–705.

Ross, L. (1977) The intuitive psychologist and his shortcomings. In Bahkowitz, L. (ed.): *Advances in Experimental Social Psychology*, Vol 10. New York: Academic Press.

Seligman, M. (1975) *Helplessness: On Depression, Development and Death*, San Francisco: W. H. Freeman.

Slovic, P. (1966) Cue consistency and cue utilization in judgement. *American Journal of Psychology*, **79**, 427–434.

Slovic, P. (1972) *From Shakespeare to Simon*. Portland: Oregon Research Institute.

Sproull, L. (1981) Beliefs in organizations. In Nyström, P. and Starbuck, W. (eds): *Handbook of Organizational Design*. New York: Oxford University Press.

Starbuck, W. H. (1976) Organizations and their environments. In Dunnette, M. D. (ed.) *Handbook of Industrial and Organizational Psychology*. Chicago: Rand McNally, 1069-123.

Starbuck, W. H., Greve, A., and Hedberg, B. L. T. (1978) Responding to crises. *Journal of Business Administration*, **9**, 111-137.

Streufert, S. (1973) Effects of information relevance on decision making in complex environments. *Memory and Cognition*, **3**, 224-228.

Tarkowsky, Z. M. (1958) Symposium: Problems in Decision making. *Operational Research Quarterly*, **9**, 121-123.

Tversky, A. and Kahneman, D. (1974) Judgement under uncertainty: heuristics and biases. *Science*, **185**, 1124-1131.

Wallach, M. A., Kogan, N., and Bem, D. J. (1962) Group influence on individual risk-taking. *Journal of Abnormal and Social Psychology*, **65**, 65-68.

Wallach, M. A., Kogan, N., and Bem, D. (1964) Diffusion of responsibility and level risk taking in groups. *Journal of abnormal and Social Psychology*, **68**, 263–274.

Weiner, B. and Kukla, A. (1970) An attributional analysis of achievement motivation. *Journal of Personality and Social Psychology*, Vol 15.

Zajonc, R. (1960) The Process of Cognitive Tuning in Communication. *Journal of Abnormal and Social Psychology*, **61** (2), 159–167.

Zander, A. (1971) *Motives and Goals in Groups*. New York: Academic Press.